Making Connections

Movement, Music, & Literacy

Related Resources from High/Scope Press

Teaching Movement & Dance: A Sequential Approach to Rhythmic Movement, Sixth Edition

Round the Circle: Key Experiences in Movement for Young Children, Second Edition

High/Scope Preschool Key Experience Series: Movement and Music (Booklet and video/DVD set)

Movement Plus Music: Activities for Children Ages 3 to 7, Third Edition

Movement in Steady Beat — Learning on the Move, Ages 3 to 7, Second Edition

Rhythmically Moving 1–9 (CDs)

85 Engaging Movement Activities — Learning on the Move, K–6

Movement Plus Rhymes, Songs, & Singing Games, Second Edition

Available from
High/Scope® Press
A division of the High/Scope Educational Research Foundation
600 N. River St., Ypsilanti, MI 48198-2898
Orders: 800/40-PRESS, Fax 800/442-4FAX
press@highscope.org; Online *www.highscope.org*

LEARNING ON THE MOVE
Preschool-Grade 2

Making Connections

Movement, Music, & Literacy

Lizabeth Haraksin-Probst,
Janet Hutson-Brandhagen,
and Phyllis S. Weikart

HIGHSCOPE
PRESS®

Ypsilanti, Michigan

Published by

High/Scope® Press
A division of the
High/Scope Educational Research Foundation
600 North River Street
Ypsilanti, Michigan 48198-2898
(734)485-2000, fax (734)485-0704
press@highscope.org
www.highscope.org

Editor: Marcella Weiner, *High/Scope Press Editor*

Design and Production: Judy Seling of Seling Design

Photography:
Jennifer Burd — 112 (top and right)
Gregory Fox — 2, 3, 4, 6, 9, 15, 17, 21, 23, 25, 39 (top), 41, 45, 56, 59, 67, 73, 83, 90, 97, 101, 102, 108, 112 (left), 115, 140 (top)
Suzanne Gainsley — 145
Lizabeth Haraksin-Probst — 39 (bottom), 53, 55, 63
Janet Hutson-Brandhagen — 37, 65, 71, 79, 80, 99, 140 (bottom), 165 (top right and middle)

Library of Congress Cataloging-in-Publication Data
Haraksin-Probst, Lizabeth.
  Making connections : movement, music & literacy / Lizabeth
Haraksin-Probst, Janet Hutson-Brandhagen, and Phyllis S. Weikart.
    p. cm.
  Includes index.
  ISBN-13: 978-1-57379-319-3 (soft cover : alk. paper) 1. Reading
readiness. 2. Music in education. 3. Movement education. I.
Hutson-Brandhagen, Janet. II. Weikart, Phyllis S., 1931- III. Title.
  LB1525.6.H37 2007
  372.41'4--dc22
                                    2007034029

Printed in the United States of America
10 9 8 7 6 5 4 3

CONTENTS

ACKNOWLEDGMENTS

We extend our heartfelt gratitude to the following people.

Our professional colleagues:

- Karen Sawyers, director of Movement and Music at High/Scope, for her vision on this project, for the time she spent working with us, and for encouraging us to work toward this goal — not always an easy job!

- The teachers in the Education Through Movement network, who are part of a national network committed to helping children and adults attain success academically, artistically, musically, and physically.

- Craig Newby and Karen Sullivan, whose kindness and encouragement continue to help Liz each and every day; Judy Kerwin, whose wisdom, understanding of how children learn, and sense of humor is so appreciated; Bob Stilwell, who introduced Liz to the most magical world of kindergarten and whose mentorship is priceless; Stephanie Lance, for lengthy conversations about curriculum concepts, early childhood principles, and child development that have been instrumental in the development of the ideas in this book; Nancy Carteen, for her suggestion of "stepping stones" and her encouragement; Lori Campos, for digging up supportive articles and research to share; Shawn Barksdale and Karen Jacobs, as inspirational partners; Linda Lovett and Cindy Gardner, for modeling what High/Scope can do for children as teachers of Liz's own children, Emily and Jonathan.

- Jan Delacy, the Director of Instruction (now retired) and principals Mike McBride, George MacDonald, and Evan Collins, administrators in the Bellevue Public Schools, for their words of encouragement to Janet, their keen observations, and for their high praise for how the students were constructing their own knowledge by using this teaching approach.

- The High/Scope publications staff, for making our cauldron of experiences and refining them into something worth sharing with others: Nancy Brickman, Director of Publications, Marcella Weiner, our editor; and Pattie McDonald, our editorial assistant.

Our friends and our families:

- Dr. Wolin, Liz's "personal angel," and Laura Ikenberry, her "garden friend"; Little Church from The Grove: Becky, Dick, Jenn, Darryl, for their constant love, prayers, vigilance, "garden friendship," and encouragement; and Chandler, for being a trouper; Deanna and Otto Probst, Liz's model in-laws, for listening and loving the entire family; Phyllis and John Haraksin, who taught Liz that nothing is impossible; sisters Julie, who looks for every opportunity to live life to its fullest and make each day really count, and Mimi, who listens without judgment; Aunt Chris and Aunt Joyce, who were great listeners and encouragers and always there. Most of all, thanks to Liz's children and husband: Emily, whose sweet, sensitive, caring disposition brings joy to a mother's heart; Jonathan, who challenges and tests and is always there for a good back rub, foot massage, and a hug; and Steve, Liz's love, inspiration, encourager, God's gift, "I must have done something good!"

- Janet's parents, who were both educators and instilled that love of learning in their students and in their family; brother Phil and sisters Meredith and Claudia Jo, who have been there for all of Janet's endeavors; Gordon, Janet's husband, and their two sons, Eric and Paul, and

Paul's delightful wife, Lise, for being a constant source of love and care and for being understanding when Janet was gone from home for workshops. When she retired from public school teaching, Eric asked his mother about what she did in Movement and Music workshops, and, as she explained, he smiled and said, "It's nice that you still have a job where you can play, Mom."

- Dave Weikart, Phyllis's late husband; her daughters, Cindy, Cathy, Jenny, and Gretchen; and sons-in-law, Dale, Mark, and Vince for support and understanding over the years.

— Lizabeth Haraksin-Probst, Janet Hutson-Brandhagen, and Phyllis S. Weikart

THE STEPPING STONES TO LITERACY

A child sits up…when a child is ready to sit up.
A child crawls…when a child is ready to crawl.
A child walks…when a child is ready to walk.
A child talks…when a child is ready to talk.

Childhood milestones are attained when the child has observed the action modeled many times, received encouragement in previous attempts, gained enough strength, and acquired the necessary underlying experiences to allow these milestones to happen without pressure. The child is not being taught; instead, the child reaches the milestone naturally, given a stimulating, motivating, and supportive environment. In much the same manner as a child learns how to sit, crawl, walk, and talk, a child needs to be in a supportive environment to naturally develop the skills needed for reaching the next milestone: language, reading, writing.

Our adult world revolves around language and literacy skills, including reading and writing. Reading and writing represent so many abstract cognitive processes that we think of them as skills that need to be taught. We forget to support children's foundational experiences, the stepping stones to language and literacy, beginning at very simple levels of understanding, joining them at their developmental level, and then providing support for their new understandings and knowledge.

The "Education Through Movement: Building the Foundation" program incorporates the **movement-based active learning process** (see p. 2 for more information), where the teachers help create these foundational experiences for children. In the movement-based active learning process, children have the opportunity to work in depth with a concept or skill by using their bodies and adding language and sound (including voice) before applying it to printed text.

Children who are actively involved in the movement-based active learning process have more opportunities to experience language in a very concrete manner with their bodies. These concrete experiences are essential for children's understanding as they begin to work with abstract concepts. Let's take a look at how these abstract concepts can be brought to a concrete level by having children use their bodies as the materials for understanding.

Awareness of sound comes through purposeful use of sound in a child's work and play environment, so he or she understands the many possibilities of sound and how sounds are made. This awareness provides a foundation for phonological and phonemic awareness. Through purposeful use, children approximate the sounds they hear using their own voices, representing them with movement, and share the sound and movement with other children. Have you ever been with children when a fire engine with its siren blaring passes by? The children naturally begin to represent the fire truck with movement and sound, using their bodies and voice to create a concrete representation of what they just heard.

When children approximate sounds and represent them with movement, they share their sound and movement with other children. They also are encouraged to talk about what the mouth and voice do to make the sound. Exploration and purposeful work with producing sound strengthens muscles of the mouth, which helps develop clear articulation. Children discover the positions of the tongue and lips and the inner shape of the mouth as they make a particular sound. When children are face to face with a speaker, they can hear clearly and can watch the different shapes of the speaker's mouth. Observing mouth formations enhances articulation.

Sharing and describing purposeful movements in a supportive environment helps children develop language skills as well as self-confidence.

These concrete experiences focus on details and thus should precede connecting the sounds to abstract letter sounds. Aural discrimination, which is very abstract, is a precursor to rhyming, alliteration, writing, and reading. Carefully planned opportunities that incorporate the child (body, voice, and brain) provide these foundational experiences and create an environment for success with language and literacy. The movement-based active learning process, which the activities in this book are based on and is described next, helps teachers create these carefully planned opportunities that help bring abstract concepts to a concrete level.

A Movement-Based Active Learning Process

The movement-based active learning process includes an approach to teaching and learning that stresses process as well as content. In this learning process, *learners and teachers are partners* — mutual initiators and supporters of learning. The **movement core, the Teaching Model,** and **active learning support strategies,** three components of the movement-based active learning process, are described here. For a more complete description of this process, see *Round the Circle: Key Experiences in Movement for Young Children.*[1]

Tying shoes is a nonlocomotor (also called anchored) movement that children do every day.

---

[1]Phyllis S. Weikart, *Round the Circle: Key Experiences in Movement for Young Children,* 2nd ed. (Ypsilanti, MI: High/Scope Press, 2000).

Movement Core

The movement core is a summary of the motor developmental base for purposeful movement for all ages in the "Education Through Movement: Building the Foundation" program. Note that one of the movement core diagrams is labeled "nonlocomotor" while the other is labeled "locomotor." In each diagram, the text inside the circle refers to the way the body can be organized for purposeful movement.

Each diagram illustrates the progression of movement complexity from the top to the bottom of the circle — with the easiest movements at the top and the most complex at the bottom. As teachers introduce movement to children of any age, these progressions from simple to complex should be kept in mind. As the diagram indicates, "two sides" (moving both arms symmetrically), is the easiest pattern when using nonlocomotor movement, movement of the upper body. "Alternating sides" is the easiest pattern when using locomotor movement. "One side... other side" refers to movements repeated on one side of the body and then on the other side. For nonlocomotor movement, movements are easiest to follow when both

Jumping is a locomotor (also called nonanchored) movement.

sides of the body are moving symmetrically. (Nonlocomotor movement refers to anchored movement, such as bending, twisting, rocking, or swinging one's arms.) Moving one side in repetition followed by the other side is more difficult, and alternating sides is the most difficult of these movement patterns. For locomotor movement, alternating sides is the easiest pattern, followed by two sides (e.g., jumping), followed by one side in repetition (e.g., hopping). (Locomotor movement refers to nonanchored movement, such as running, jumping, and hopping.)

The words placed around the circle of each movement core diagram refer to the ways that the body executes purposeful movement. **Single** movements are those that can be labeled with one word spoken over and over (e.g., "March, march, march, march"). **Sequenced** movements have two or more labels (e.g., "Bend, straighten; bend, straighten"). **Single** movements are easier than **sequenced** movements. **Static** movements stop or pause before a new movement is presented (e.g., both hands begin on the knees and then go to the shoulders or head). **Dynamic** movements continue without pausing (e.g., both hands begin on the knees and then pat on the knees several times). **Static** movements are easier than **dynamic** ones.

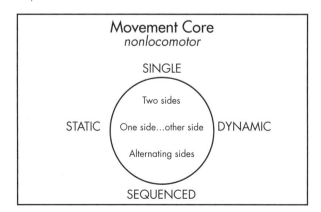

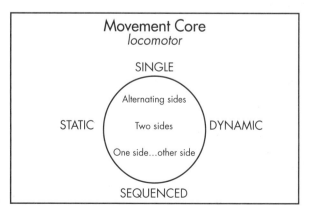

Teaching Model

The recommended method for presenting the activities in this book is the **Teaching Model,** which is the second component of the movement-based active learning process. The Teaching Model has three parts: **separate** (demonstrate *or* tell *or* use hands-on guidance), **simplify** (begin with what is easy or manageable to learn), and **facilitate** (help children think about and describe their movement). Educators have found the model's three parts can lead to increased success, to a sense of responsibility in learners, and to a decreased need to reteach concepts after they have been introduced. Let's take a closer look at each of the parts to see why such favorable results occur.

Using the separate component of the teaching model, this teacher demonstrates how she is moving an object.

Separate. This part involves initiating experiences or presenting information by using only one mode of presentation at a time: demonstration, verbal directions, **or** hands-on guidance. By choosing to **separate** (i.e, use only one of these three modes of presentation at a time), you enable the children to focus on a single message. Combining two or modes of presentation, such as telling while showing, usually gives children too much sensory input and some children may miss the information entirely because of the confusion of using two senses at once. It is important, however, to maintain an appropriate balance between the different modes of presentation.

Simplify. This part involves beginning with what is easy or manageable to process, so all children can become immediately engaged and experience success. To **simplify,** first consider the children's present capabilities and determine the subtasks that make up the task, using knowledge of prerequisite skills. Taking these factors into account, determine which subtasks are appropriate to the development level of the children and begin there. Although you may be concerned that the **simplify** strategy will slow you down, we have found this part well worth the extra few minutes required because it often results in our children attaining true ownership of concepts.

Facilitate. The first two parts of the Teaching Model (**separate and simplify**) are strategies you can use in presenting concepts and in planning and initiating activities. The third part of the Teaching Model — **facilitate** — concerns the ways you engage children through action, thought, and language to support them in constructing their own knowledge. You **facilitate** when you encourage and support children in initiating their own ideas and when you give them time to explore concepts on their own, with partners, or in small groups, planning and making choices about how they will solve problems. You also **facilitate** when you encourage descriptive language from children and when the children listen and respond to the language they use among themselves. Finally, providing a safe, interactive environment where you and the children can work as partners is the most important way you can **facilitate** the learning process.

So far we have examined the movement core and the Teaching Model. We now turn to the final component: active learning support strategies.

Active Learning Support Strategies

Dictionary definitions of "teach" often include phrases like "to impart knowledge or skills" or "to show or help to learn." Of these phrases, the most significant to us is "help to learn." These words describe the teacher's facilitative role in an environment that supports active learning. The teacher's role, then, is to transform children from passive receivers of information to active constructors of their own knowledge. When teaching is approached in this way, children become absorbed in their learning tasks and usually display an energy and zeal that are often lacking in teacher-directed classrooms.

The following are basic strategies of High/Scope's active learning approach that support such a dynamic learning environment:

- *Initiation by you and the children* is critical to successful learning. When children's ideas are incorporated in the experience, you will find that children generally maintain high interest. Furthermore, the ideas that are mutually generated far surpass those generated by you alone.
- *Exploration of purposeful movement and sound* leads to true understanding and the ability to apply curriculum concepts. This kind of exploration involves thought and intention rather than random activity.
- *Choices and planning by children* enable them to be actively involved in the learning process. Children take on ownership of the task and its solutions.
- *Language listened to and supplied* implies much verbal interaction as children verbally describe and suggest movements and sounds and listen to others do so. An important teacher strategy is to reinforce with language many of the things children are doing, which helps children in developing cognitive understanding. By supplying language, you also help children transfer learning to make associations from existing knowledge to new knowledge.
- *Reflection* encourages children to learn by thinking back on their experiences and helps you determine if further experiences are necessary for the children to achieve ownership of a particular concept.
- *Support from you and children's peers* implies the creation of a supportive environment in which children feel they have a say in their own learning. Providing a positive, supportive classroom atmosphere means realizing that you and the children are on this educational journey together.

In this section, we have described three important components of High/Scope's movement-based active learning approach. Taken together, the movement core, Teaching Model, and active learning support strategies constitute a method you can use to inspire or lead from behind. The next section we call "Steps to Success" (otherwise known as very practical suggestions) that will help you successfully use this method to implement the activities in this book and make reading and writing come alive for the children you teach.

STEPS TO SUCCESS

Make sure that children are comfortable. Have children stand in a loose formation, rather than a circle or a line, so that children can be anonymous when working in their personal space, making sounds and doing actions at the same time as the other children. This allows for children to express themselves more readily when using exploration and problem solving.

Have children explore concepts before sharing ideas. Exploration is the time for children to try to figure out how they can move their bodies or manipulate materials. Children try on their own; describe what they did; and share with a partner, a small group, or the whole group. This strategy is essential for the learners, as it assists learners to achieve success, and for you, as you observe the child's previous knowledge and understanding, providing insight for future planning. Exploration also assists to create an environment in which children are confident they will be respected and afforded the courtesy to work through possibilities before being asked to share their ideas.

Encourage children to share their ideas. When children share their ideas, movements, and plans, a supportive environment is created. Children are more motivated to try what their peers can do rather than what you might lead. Here also lies an opportunity for children to discuss with each other strategies to help them be successful: Children are learning from each other. You can support learners through facilitation and clarification to support new understanding and skills.

Have children share out loud. It is important for each child to respond — hearing one's own voice; feeling the shape of the mouth and placement of the teeth and tongue; hearing one's own descriptions, ideas, plans, and choices stated *out loud*. Often these *out loud* discussions happen with children all answering at once, where you may not hear all the responses but every child has brought his or her ideas to language. This out loud response aids in long-term retention. The "talking about," "describing," and "explaining how" parts of the activities are facilitation and reflective pieces that bring the movement to cognition, providing opportunities for children to talk about their experiences and awareness. Reflection also helps you determine if further experiences are necessary to achieve ownership of a particular concept.

Use movement first. Movement should always occur first. This provides an opportunity for children to deal with the motor component in isolation before adding a rhyme, song, or recording. When using recorded music to lead steady beat, locomotor movement, nonlocomotor movement, or movement patterns, children are generally more successful if they have worked through the movements in the following progression:

- One's own timing (no music) using SAY & DO (where a child says the label of the word-related movement and simultaneously performs a related movement, e.g., pat, pat, pat, pat)
- With a partner (no music) while using the SAY & DO strategy for synchronization and one-to-one correspondence
- With the group (no music) matching a few different children's steady beat tempos
- With the group in common time, in the approximate tempo of the music, using SAY & DO
- With the music

After children learn the movement pattern on their own, they can do it with a partner (when appropriate) while using SAY & DO.

There is one exception: When children are intuitively responding to the music, when their movement is to be a response to the music itself, the music needs to come first.

Incorporate steady beat. Mother Goose nursery rhymes are wonderfully appropriate for incorporating steady beat, and there are a wealth of resources available that offer interesting rhymes and poetry appropriate for older children. By using steady beat in different ways, children develop basic timing skills, and as they develop these skills, you will observe more fluency in speech and reading. Use appropriate selections of poetry, based on children's interest and age, to support steady beat, rhyme, repetition, flow of speech, and memorization.

> **Steady beat** is the consistent repetitive pulse that lies within every rhyme, song, or musical selection.

For steady beat movements in the upper body (e.g., patting your legs with your hands), use a steady beat that is a comfortable rocking beat. Dr. Edwin Gordon, a music theorist, has termed this the *macrobeat*. For steady beat movements in the feet (e.g., marching), use a steady beat that is a comfortable marching or walking beat for the children, which Dr. Gordon calls the *microbeat*.[2] There are two microbeats to every macrobeat, or two marches for each rocking motion, as shown here:

PAT	PAT	PAT	PAT
ROCK	ROCK	ROCK	ROCK
MARCH MARCH	MARCH MARCH	MARCH MARCH	MARCH MARCH

To incorporate steady beat in learning new rhymes or saying familiar rhymes, use the following steps:

- *Learning new rhymes.* Children start a movement in steady beat that is quiet. As the leader, synchronize the movement for the children by using an anchor word for each movement (e.g., "Beat, beat, beat, listen" or "Pat, pat, pat, listen" or "March, march, march, listen"). Speak the rhyme in the natural flow of speech while the children keep the steady beat.
- *Learning all the phrases of new rhymes.* Children start a movement in steady beat. As the leader, synchronize the movement by adding an anchor word for each movement (e.g., "Beat, beat, beat, speak"). Speak the first phrase of the rhyme several times, and encourage the children to join as they feel comfortable with the rhyme. Use the same process, and speak the first and second phrase of the rhyme several times, again encouraging children to join in as they feel comfortable. Use the same process to learn the third phrase and then the third and fourth phrases. Use the same process and speak the entire rhyme several times as a class.
- *Saying familiar rhymes.* Children start a movement in steady beat. As the leader, synchronize the movement by adding an anchor word for each movement (e.g., "Beat, beat, beat, speak"). As a class, say the rhyme together.

Offer open-ended tasks. Support divergent thinking and problem solving by setting up tasks so there are many possibilities for many different responses. Avoid the "right" or "wrong" answer, and have children respond in complete sentences whenever possible.

Involve the children in planning. Planning involves problem solving, being purposeful, and making decisions about choices. When children have choices about how they plan and how they carry out their plan, they have ownership. Planning helps children focus on concepts so that the intention is stated and the child's trial-and-error problem solving can lead to new learning and understanding.

---

[2]Edwin Gordon, *Learning Sequences in Music* (Chicago: GIA Publishing, 2003).

Ensure that children are working actively. When the children have made a plan and stated their intentions, the movement is purposeful. Active, yes! Everyone could do different things at one time. It might be noisy, but not chaotic. Children also are accountable for their actions as they share their movement plans with others.

Have children lead. All children need the opportunity to *voluntarily* lead and share. This sharing validates each child's ideas and builds confidence. Children will learn more when they take the risk to be the leader.

Support a language-rich environment. Encourage children to use complete sentences to communicate their thoughts and to listen to one another when sharing ideas, labeling actions and movements and what they represent, and comparing and contrasting their ways of moving. Interaction of children with other children (as well as with adults) is especially beneficial for English language learners and children with special needs, because other children and adults can supply the vocabulary or labels needed for language acquisition.

Start the music from the beginning of the recording. When children are sharing a movement idea, start the recording from the beginning so each child has the introduction, thus giving the child time to listen to the tempo before starting the movement.

Use instrumental music. Instrumental music lets the listener focus on the musical elements. If there are lyrics (words or vocals), the attention naturally goes to the language. Use instrumental music (without words or vocals) so children can focus on the steady beat, instrumentation, form, melody, and so forth.

Sing songs. Use your voice, not a CD. When you are the musical source, you can adjust the tempo of the song to the task, the children's tempos, how high or low they can sing it comfortably, or the ability level of your group. The CD in the back of this book is provided for you to learn the songs. Recordings are abstract, and children cannot see the musicians or watch the mouth of the singer. Children will be encouraged to sing when they see and hear it modeled by you. Use the following tips when singing songs in your class:

- *Introducing new songs.* Children start a movement in steady beat. As the leader, synchronize the movement for the children by using an anchor word for each movement (e.g., "Beat, beat, beat, listen" or "Pat, pat, pat, listen" or "March, march, march, listen"). Sing the song on a neutral syllable, such as "bah" or "la," as modeled on the enclosed CD. This **simplify** strategy provides the children the opportunity to listen to the melody. After repeating the melody using a neutral syllable several times, encourage the children to join in as they feel comfortable with the melody. Then, after they feel comfortable with the melody, have the children once again start a movement in steady beat. Synchronize the movement for the group by using an anchor word (e.g., "Beat, beat, beat, listen"). This time, sing the song with the words while the children keep the steady beat.
- *Learning all phrases of new songs.* Children start a movement in steady beat. Synchronize the movement for the children by adding the anchor pitch sung on the beginning pitch of the song (e.g.,"Beat, beat, beat, sing"). Sing the first phrase of the song several times. Encourage the children to join in as they feel comfortable with the song. Use the same process, and sing the first and second phrases of the song several times. Use the same process to learn the third phrase and then the third and fourth phrases. Use the same process and sing the entire song several times as a class.
- *Singing familiar songs together.* Children start a movement in steady beat. Synchronize the movement for the children by adding the anchor pitch sung on the beginning pitch of the song (e.g., "Beat, beat, beat, and sing" or "One, two, sing with me"), and sing the song together.

Sing in your head voice. Children have short vocal chords and will sing in tune more easily when you pitch songs in their higher range. As an adult, you may need to call the cat ("Here kitty, kitty") to feel that place in your voice that is best for children and lead from there.

Be a partner with children. Participate with the children, and try their ideas. Facilitate the learning to bring concepts to a higher level of understanding. Don't be surprised if some of the movement plans and patterns children lead are difficult for you as an adult. If you can't do the cartwheel that is suggested by a child, you need to acknowledge its difficulty and support each child's expertise.

We now invite you to become a partner with the children in your class using this process to enjoy the magic of children playing with literacy concepts and skills to become competent readers and writers and enthusiastic learners.

ACTIVITY ELEMENTS

The activities contained in this book bring language and literacy alive with fun, motivating, and thought-provoking teacher-initiated active learning experiences. Watch for opportunities to support child-initiated learning as well.

Before attempting the activities, we recommend reading the preceding pages, which describe components of the **movement-based active learning process.** We hope our suggestions will give you a way to begin to work within the framework of the movement-based active learning process and that these activities will become a part of the total educational approach used in your classroom or home.

For older children, bringing oral language to print is an important step to becoming a confident writer.

Each activity contains the following elements:

- **Grade Level:** The activities are clearly labeled in the top left-hand corner by

  PRESCHOOL–GRADE 2   or   K–GRADE 2

- **Curriculum Concepts:** The curriculum concepts listed are for *movement and music* and *literacy.*
- **Description:** A brief description of the activity is given in italics.
- **Materials:** This part lists all the materials you will need for the activity. Materials needed for the Extensions are also included here. Some of the activities use musical selections recorded on the enclosed CD. This CD is a teaching tool for you — to help you learn the songs so that you can, in turn, sing the songs to and with the children.
- **Steps to Success:** Suggested steps to follow in presenting the activity are described in this section. Although each activity is written as a progressive experience, you may wish to omit some steps or to include others not listed, depending on the environment and ability levels of the children in your class. **We urge you to always include the exploration phase (Step 1) of the activity no matter the age level that you are working with.** Some of the later steps in the activities may be appropriate for older children and the appropriate grade level is indicated before the step (e.g., Grades 1–2).

    Often a step will incorporate the teacher or children to bring their oral language to print. This is essential in supporting young learners as they begin to make a conscious connection that their spoken words can be represented as text. It also encourages the older children to write down their own ideas, an important step to becoming a confident writer.

- **Facilitation and Reflection:** This section contains sample questions you may pose. The specific questions you use, of course, will depend on the age and experience of the children. You do not need to ask all of them. Including these questions is based on our philosophy that *thought* and *language* must be added to action to help children reach true ownership of language and literacy concepts while using movement and music.
- **Extensions:** These are suggested ways to expand or modify the activity. Many of these Extensions come directly from our children's suggestions; others are from what we have observed children doing as they use alternative materials and strategies. The grade or age level is indicated if the Extension is more appropriate for a specific age or grade level.

◆ ◆ ◆

ACTIVITIES

ATTRIBUTES OF SHAPES

Children explore the attributes of shapes through movement.

MATERIALS

★ Large felt shapes (circles, triangles, rectangles, squares), one for each
child in the class

★ "Sauerländer Quadrille," "Soldier's Joy," or "The Sally Gardens" on the
enclosed CD

★ CD player

STEPS TO SUCCESS

Preschool–Grade 2

Step 1
With their arms out in front of them, ask the children to draw, in slow
motion, straight lines, curved lines, and letters that they know in their personal space. Then ask them to draw any shapes they know using their
arms out in front of them.

Step 2
Randomly place felt shapes on the floor, and ask the children to choose a
shape to work with. Have children explore ways to go around the edges
of their chosen shape that is on the floor. For example, children may trace
the shape with their foot, jump around the shape, or march around the
shape. Ask the children to tell someone near what they notice about the
shape they have chosen, and have them identify felt shapes on the floor
that are the same as their shape.

Step 3

Play an instrumental selection (such as "Soldier's Joy") from the enclosed CD. Ask the children to plan a movement to travel to the steady beat of the music until the music stops. For example, children may make one of the following plans:

1. Go to a shape that is the same color.

2. Go to one that is a different color.

3. Go to one that has only straight sides.

4. Go to one that has four corners.

The focus is not on the names of the shapes, but their attributes. Encourage the children to talk about the details that they notice about the shapes.

FACILITATION AND REFLECTION

★ What are some of the things you noticed about one of the shapes?

★ What was your movement plan for traveling to the steady beat of the music?

★ What are the attributes of your favorite shape?

★ How did you travel to the new shapes when the music stopped?

★ How did you decide which shape to go to?

EXTENSIONS

Preschool–Grade 2

★ Instead of shapes on the floor, use letters, numbers, or colors, and repeat the steps in this activity.

★ Have children use their singing voice to describe their shape or their movement plan.

2

Book Sharing

Children listen to the teacher reading a book and act out their favorite character with movement and sound. Older children choose a book of their own and share the movement and sound of a character in their book with a partner.

Movement & Music Curriculum Concepts
- Expressing creativity in movement
- Moving in locomotor ways

Literacy Curriculum Concepts
- Listening to stories and poems
- Retelling
- Sharing literature

Materials

★ Books appropriate for emergent readers (that is, books that have a predictable text, repeating text, few words on a page, or illustrations that depict the text)

Steps to Success

Preschool–Grade 2

Step 1
Reread a favorite book, such as *Brown Bear, Brown Bear, What Do You See?* by Bill Martin, Jr.; *Barnyard Dance* by Sandra Boynton; *Sometimes I Like to Curl Up in a Ball* by Vicki Churchill and Charles Fuge; and *My Many Colored Days* by Dr. Seuss. Have the children suggest a favorite character from the book and explore how this character would move and sound. Have them share, copy, describe, and compare and contrast this character's movement and sound. Choose other characters as appropriate. (Older children may want to choose their own favorite character and make a plan to move and sound like that character. Encourage the children to share their plans with partners.)

Step 2

Ask each child to choose a book they know well. Have the children work with a partner and take turns talking about each page of the book. Encourage them to tell the story of the pictures in a singing voice.

Step 3

Ask the children to choose a favorite page in their book. Have them represent that page with movement and sound and share this with their partner.

Our love of literature can be shared with children through our enthusiasm.

Facilitation and Reflection

★ What was your favorite character? Why?

★ How did you move? How did you sound?

★ What part of the story did you show?

★ Why did you choose that part of the story?

★ How were your books the same/different from the other children's books?

Extensions

Preschool-Grade 2

★ Have the children look for letters from their name and words that they know in the text of their book.

K-Grade 2

★ Have the children find a new partner and share their movement and sound from their chosen book.

★ Let children bring their chosen book home to share with their family.

CONVERSATIONS SUNG ON RANDOM PITCHES

Children respond, retell, and describe using their singing voice, which supports expressive speech, storytelling, and expressive reading.

Movement & Music Curriculum Concepts
- Exploring the singing voice
- Singing in random pitches

Literacy Curriculum Concepts
- Listening to stories and poems
- Making up stories and rhymes
- Predicting what may happen next in a book or story

MATERIALS

★ "Random Pitch Singing" on the enclosed CD

★ CD player

★ Book-making materials (Extensions)

STEPS TO SUCCESS

Preschool–Grade 2

Step 1

Sing a random pitch song. At the end of the story, sing "The end," and ask the children to sing a response in random pitches. For example, after a field trip to the zoo, you could sing, "Yesterday we went to the zoo. What do you see?" Children could then respond by singing about all the animals they saw: "We saw bears, lions, and tigers." Then respond with singing "The end." Listen to "Random Pitch Singing" on the enclosed CD for an example.

Step 2

Start the random pitch singing, and have individual children respond in random pitch.

TEACHER'S TIP

Some children have not found their singing voice and will speak their response; they just need more experience with their voice to be able to sing on their own. As a safety net, when you hear children finishing their random pitch song, sing "The end" so that children are not singing alone.

FACILITATION AND REFLECTION

★ What does your voice do differently when you sing your story instead of speaking it?

★ When else might you sing random pitch stories or songs?

EXTENSIONS

Preschool–Grade 2

★ Sing directions for the children in random pitches so they get more experience hearing the use of the singing voice.

★ Make a class book of the random pitch stories that were done orally so that the children can sing them again in their own way.

★ Sing familiar stories, such as *Brown Bear, Brown Bear* (by Eric Carle and Bill Martin), "The Three Bears," "The Three Little Pigs," and other stories you know.

By exploring his singing voice, this child is developing his language and music skills at the same time.

CREATING MY OWN SONG

Children use words creatively by making up lines in a song. They listen to and act upon movement directions.

Movement & Music Curriculum Concepts
- Acting upon movement directions
- Moving in nonloco-motor ways
- Responding to verbal directions

Literacy Curriculum Concepts
- Rewriting a song
- Using positional words

MATERIALS

★ "One, Two, Three" on the enclosed CD
★ CD player

STEPS TO SUCCESS

Preschool–Grade 2

Step 1

Sing "One, Two, Three," and ask the children to add the last word, making up as many endings as there is time. (This activity is good for transition times so that children are working on focusing.) See the sidebar for Learning New Songs for tips on introducing new songs; this approach is demonstrated on the enclosed CD.

In this activity you will only sing the directions, while the children show the movement or body part. This is an example of the **separate** strategy, where you are using one mode of presentation at a time.

Learning New Songs

Have children start a movement in steady beat (e.g., quietly patting their legs). Synchronize the movement by using an anchor word for each beat (e.g., "Beat, beat, beat, beat"). While keeping steady beat, say "Beat, beat, beat, listen," and sing the melody on a neutral syllable such as "bahm." Sing the melody several times on a neutral syllable, encouraging children to join in as they feel comfortable. Sing "Beat, beat, ready to sing" using the beginning pitch of the song (as demonstrated on the enclosed CD), and ask the children to join in, singing the song at least four times.

One, Two, Three

Lizabeth Haraksin-Probst

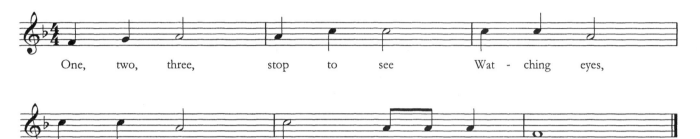

One, two, three, stop to see Wat - ching eyes, lis - tening ears, Hands o - ver my head.

Step 2

Ask the children what they would do or sing if they used a body part in relationship to an object. Use positional words, for example, *hands over the table* or *feet under the chair*. Using the children's examples, sing the song again, while the children follow the song's directions.

Grade 2

Step 3

Sing "One, Two, Three," replacing the last line of the song with two-step directions, as shown below. Have the children wait until the two directions are sung before acting upon the directions.

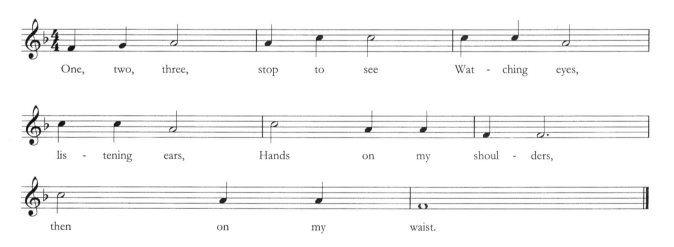

One, two, three, stop to see Wat - ching eyes, lis - tening ears, Hands on my shoul - ders, then on my waist.

FACILITATION AND REFLECTION

★ How did you decide what body part to use?

★ What were some of the positional words used?

CREATING PATHWAYS

After exploring how to move in different pathways, children use long pieces of yarn to make different pathways and letter shapes.

MATERIALS

★ 7-foot or 8-foot lengths of yarn

★ *Crictor* by Tomi Ungerer (Extensions)

★ Play dough (Extensions)

★ Cooked spaghetti, wax paper, string, and wire hangers (Extensions)

STEPS TO SUCCESS

K-Grade 2

Step 1
Ask the children to move in straight, curved, and zigzag pathways through the room or outside.

Step 2
Have the children combine pathways (a curved pathway with a straight pathway). Ask volunteers to share their pathways, and have the rest of the class copy and describe the pathways.

Step 3
Pass out the long yarn lengths, and ask the children to combine straight, curved, and zigzag pathways with the yarn to create letter shapes.

Step 4

Encourage the children to explore which body parts they can use to trace their letter shapes and to plan ways to travel their letter shapes. Have them describe and compare/contrast the pathways and the combinations on similar letters.

Facilitation and Reflection

★ Which pathways were the easiest for you to make?

★ Where do you find these kinds of pathways in your everyday life?

★ What was the difference between tracing your letter shapes and traveling your letter shapes?

Extensions

K–Grade 2

★ Read *Crictor,* by Tomi Ungerer, where a snake helps a teacher in her classroom by forming his body into letter shapes. Have children use play dough to make snakes to form pathways in the shapes of letters.

★ Cooked spaghetti lengths can be used to form letter pathways. Lay the letters on wax paper to dry and harden, and then have the children make name mobiles or spelling-word mobiles with these spaghetti letters.

This child was exploring how to make a pathway when he realized that he had made a letter: an S!

6

DOING THINGS IN SEQUENCE

Children use movement to represent a sequence of events and then write about and illustrate their sequence of events. They put their sequence of events out of order and work with classmates to put it in a logical order.

Movement & Music Curriculum Concepts
- Describing movement
- Moving in locomotor ways
- Moving in nonlocomotor ways

Literacy Curriculum Concepts
- Sequencing
- Writing in various ways: drawing, scribbling, and using letter-like forms, invented spelling, and conventional forms

MATERIALS

★ Paper for children to write on

★ Writing instruments (pencils, markers, crayons, etc.)

★ Digital camera (Extensions)

STEPS TO SUCCESS

K–Grade 2

Step 1
Ask the children to choose a sequence of events to represent through movement, such as the sequence of events for getting ready for school (e.g., wake up [stretching], get up [jumping out of bed], shower [washing body], get dressed [pretending to put on clothes], eat breakfast [pretending to eat], and go to school [running]).

Step 2
Have the children write down the sequence of events on separate pieces of paper and then illustrate the events.

Step 3
Have the children put the sentences with illustrations from Step 2 out of order. Ask them to represent the out-of-order sequence through movement to a partner or the whole group. Have the partner or group decide why this is not a logical sequence of events (e.g., it would not be logical

to get dressed before taking a shower). Have them reorder the sentences with illustrations until they find an order that can work logically and represent the sequence in movement to show the correct order.

FACILITATION AND REFLECTION

★ What did you choose as your sequence?

★ When the sequence was in a logical order, how did that affect your movement representation? What about when the sequence was not in a logical order?

★ What other things need to be completed in a logical sequence (e.g., getting ready for a soccer game)?

This girl is representing the sequence of getting ready for school (she is stretching) through movement.

EXTENSIONS

K-Grade 2

★ Take digital pictures of sequences (e.g., fixing hair, brushing teeth, cooking, getting dressed, building a snowman). After printing out the pictures, have the children write captions and play with the order.

★ See Activity 15 (From Seed to Plant) for another activity that involves sequence.

DRAWING PATHWAYS, SHAPES, AND LETTERS

Children explore moving in different pathways and drawing shapes and letters in the air with their hands and arms.

Movement & Music Curriculum Concepts
- Exploring pathways
- Moving in nonlocomotor ways
- Moving with objects

Literacy Curriculum Concepts
- Writing in various ways: drawing, scribbling, and using letter-like forms, invented spelling, and conventional forms

MATERIALS

★ "The Sally Gardens" on the enclosed CD (K–Grade 2)

★ CD player (K–Grade 2)

★ Flashlights (Extensions)

STEPS TO SUCCESS

Preschool–Grade 2

Step 1
Ask the children to move in different pathways through the room (e.g., straight, curved, or zigzag). Ask volunteers to show their pathway while the rest of the class matches the pathway and then identifies it as a straight, curved, or zigzag pathway.

Step 2
Have the children use combinations of the pathways to move through the room (e.g., straight and curved pathways).

Step 3
Ask volunteers to share their combinations, and, as a class, copy the different combinations.

Step 4

Have the children lie down on their backs on the floor and use both hands, palms together, to draw shapes in the air. Ask the children to suggest shapes to be drawn (straight lines, circles, and so forth). Ask them to suggest letters to be drawn as if they were writing on the ceiling.

K–Grade 2

Step 5

Play "The Sally Gardens" from the enclosed CD, and ask the children to draw letters as if they were writing on the ceiling. Have the children use one hand to draw the letter on the first phrase of the song and the other hand to draw the same letter on the second phrase of the song.

FACILITATION AND REFLECTION

★ Which shapes/letters can be drawn with one continuous movement? (An *S* would be one example.)

★ Which shapes/letters take two movements? (An *X* would be one example.)

★ Which letters had both straight lines and curves? Which letters had zigzags?

EXTENSIONS

K–Grade 2

★ Have the children use other body parts to draw shapes/letters, making sure to use both sides of the body (such as left elbow and right elbow).

★ Use flashlights to draw the shapes on the ceiling with and without music. Let the children take home the flashlights and draw letters/words with their families on the ceiling or walls.

★ With a partner, have children "sandwich hands" (put their hands together by alternating each other's hands) — one child takes the lead and draws a letter in the air in front of him or her and the partner says what the letter is. Have the children switch roles.

Using a new material (in this case, flashlights) makes learning how to write letters fun and exciting.

ENDiNG PuNCTUaTiON*

Children choose and use movements to express ending punctuation and then apply these punctuation marks at the end of sentences.

MaTERiaLS

★ Sentence strips with sentences suggested by the children or that the children can read (one side of the strip should have a sentence that requires a period, while the other side should have a sentence that requires a question mark *but* leave off the punctuation)

★ Blank sentence strips

★ Markers

★ Blue painter's tape

STePS To SuCCeSS

K-Grade 2

Step 1
Have the children make a class plan for a way to represent a period at the end of a sentence (e.g., the children may plan to do a jump in place). Have them practice doing their movement (in this case, a jump) and label it "Period" each time they land. As you and the children read some of the sentence strips, have the children jump at the end of each sentence and label it "Period."

---

*This activity is most appropriate for kindergartners when they are in the second half of the school year.

Step 2

Have the children make a class plan for a way to represent a question mark at the end of a sentence (e.g., the children may plan to do a karate kick in place). Have them practice doing their movement (in this case, a karate kick) and labeling it "Question mark" each time they kick. As you and the children read the sentence strips that require a question mark, have the children do a karate kick at the end of the question and label it "Question mark."

Step 3

Have the children choose partners and then distribute the blank sentence strips to the pairs of children. Ask the partners to work together to generate a sentence needing a period for one side of a sentence strip and a question needing a question mark on the other side of the sentence strip.

Step 4

Have each set of partners present their sentence strip (one side has a "telling sentence" and the other side has an "asking sentence") to another set of two children. Have each set of partners read their own strips first, putting in the appropriate ending punctuation and movement as they read them. Then, have the two sets of partners practice saying their sentence strips together, using the appropriate ending punctuation and movement.

Step 5

Ask each pair of partners to leave the sentences they generated with the other pair. Have the partners work on the other sentence strip to determine which side needs the period and which side needs the question mark. Children can write their punctuation on blue painter's tape and stick it at the end of the sentence. (The painter's tape will be removable and reusable for more practice when working with each new set of partners and sentences.)

Step 6

Have the partners read the sentence strip, adding the punctuation through movement as they come to the end of the sentence.

Step 7

Ask the partners to justify why they made the choice they did and decide, as a group, if they agree with their choices.

Step 8

Ask both sets of partners to read and punctuate the sentence strips by adding the punctuation through movement as they come to the end of the sentence.

Step 9

Have each set of partners remove the painter's tape and take their own sentence strip to another set of partners.

Step 10

Repeat Steps 4–9 so that each set of partners get many opportunities to choose . or ?

Facilitation and Reflection

★ How did you decide on which punctuation mark to put at the end of each sentence?

★ What does your voice do at the end of a question?

ENViRONMENTAL SOUNDS

Children explore movements of something in their environment and its corresponding sound. They share their favorite sounds with each other and develop movement plans. Older students write stories that incorporate these environmental sounds.

Movement & Music Curriculum Concepts
- Approximating sounds
- Describing movement
- Moving in locomotor ways
- Moving in nonlocomotor ways

Literacy Curriculum Concepts
- Aural discrimination
- Dictating stories
- Phonemic awareness
- Sequencing
- Strengthening mouth muscles for clear articulation

MaTERiaLS

★ Chart paper or whiteboard (Grades 1–2)

★ Markers or dry-erase markers (Grades 1–2)

★ Classroom instruments (Extensions)

STEPS TO SUCCESS

Preschool–Grade 2

Step 1
Have children explore movements of something that relates to their environment (e.g., a dog, an ice cream truck, or fire truck) and approximate the sound with their voices.

Step 2
Ask for a volunteer to share his or her movement while the rest of the children copy the movement and then add sound. Ask for additional volunteers to share while the others copy. Encourage children to make associations with other things that make similar sounds, such as things that make sounds with high pitches or sounds with long duration. Have children move and approximate that sound. For example, a volunteer might move around like a bird and make a "tweet-tweet" sound. After the class copies this movement, another child might associate the high pitch of the bird with the high pitch of a kitten meowing and begin to move and meow like a kitten.

Step 3

Have children describe, compare, and contrast their movements and sounds they explored in Step 2.

Step 4

Ask for a volunteer to make a favorite sound. Have the other children listen to the sound and make a plan for movement. Have the children move while the child is making his or her favorite sound. Compare and contrast the different ways the sound was represented. Repeat with other volunteers as time allows.

Grades 1-2

Step 5

Ask for ideas for stories that incorporate a sequence of three or four of these favorite sounds (first, next, then, and last) to write a class story on chart paper or the whiteboard.

Facilitation and Reflection

★ How did your movement and sound go together?

★ What was your favorite movement and sound? Why?

★ When do you hear these sounds?

★ How did you make that sound? What shape did your mouth make? What did your tongue do?

★ How did these sounds enhance your story?

Extensions

Grades 1-2

Have children choose a classroom instrument and play it. Ask children to listen carefully to the sound of the instrument and then make a sound with their mouth that represents the approximate sound of the instrument they played.

10

EXPLORING ALLITERATION

While keeping steady beat, children sing and make up songs that use words with similar and different initial consonants.

Movement & Music Curriculum Concepts
- Expressing creativity
- Feeling and expressing steady beat
- Moving in nonlocomotor ways

Literacy Curriculum Concepts
- Rhyming
- Using alliteration

MATERIALS

★ "B A Bay," "Willaby Wallaby Woo," and "Fee Fi Fiddly I O," on the enclosed CD
★ CD player
★ Construction paper (Extensions)
★ Markers (Extensions)

STEPS TO SUCCESS

Preschool–Grade 2

Step 1
Begin steady beat by quietly patting your legs with both hands, and encourage the children to join you in this movement.

Step 2
Synchronize the beat by saying "Beat, beat, beat, beat" to get all of the children moving together with the same beat. While keeping steady beat, introduce "B A Bay" (say, e.g., "Beat, beat, beat, listen") and sing the song on a neutral syllable such as "bahm" (as demonstrated on the enclosed CD). Sing the song several times on a neutral syllable, encouraging children to join in as they feel comfortable with the melody. Using the beginning pitch of the song, introduce the song (e.g., sing "Beat, beat, ready to sing") and ask the children to join you in singing as they figure out the language pattern and melody.

TEACHER'S TIP

For steady beat movements such as patting your legs, use the **macrobeat** (rocking beat), which is half as fast as a comfortable marching or walking tempo.

B A Bay

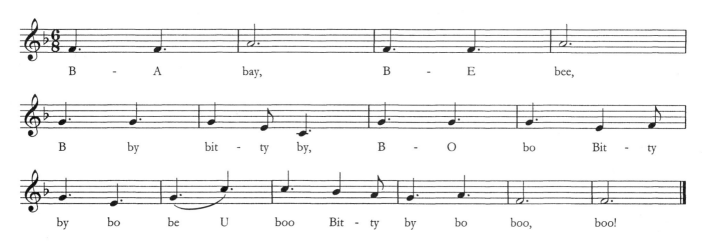

B - A bay, B - E bee, B by bit-ty by, B - O bo Bit-ty by bo be U boo Bit-ty by bo boo, boo!

Verse 2

M-A may, M-E mee,
M my mitty my, M-O mo
Mitty my mo me U moo
Mitty my mo moo, moo!

Verse 3

S-A say, S-E see,
S sy sitty sy, S-O so
Sitty sy so se U soo
Sitty sy so soo, soo!

Ask the children to suggest other consonant sounds to replace the initial /b/ (e.g., /m/, M-A may, M-E mee, M my mitty my, and so forth). Start rocking or patting the steady beat, introduce the new lyrics by singing on the starting pitch of the song (e.g., "Beat, beat, now try it with a ____)," and then sing with new lyrics.

Step 3

Introduce the following song, which can be found on the enclosed CD, following the same strategies as in Steps 1–2. Include those children's names who want to be part of the song.

Willaby Wallaby Woo

Wil - la - by wal - la - by woo An el - e - phant sat on you.

Wil - la - by wal - la - by we An el - e - phant sat on me.

Verse 2

Willaby wallaby wyllis
An elephant sat on Phyllis.
Willaby wallaby waren
An elephant sat on Karen.

Verse 3

Killaby kallaby koo
An elephant sat on you.
Killaby kallaby ke
An elephant sat on me.

Ask the children to suggest other consonant sounds to replace the /w/ (e.g., /k/, Killaby kallaby koo, an elephant sat on you, etc.). Start rocking or patting the steady beat, introduce the new lyrics by singing on the starting pitch of the song, and then sing with new lyrics.

Step 4
Introduce "Fee Fi Fiddly I O" which can be found on the enclosed CD, following the same strategies as Steps 1–2.

Fee Fi Fiddly I O
(I've Been Working on the Railroad)

Verse 2	Verse 3	Verse 4
Lee Li Liddly I O	Mee Mi Middly I O	See Si Siddly Si So
Lee Li Liddly I O-o-o-o	Mee Mi Middly I O-o-o-o	See Si Siddly Si So-o-o-o
Lee Li Liddly I O	Mee Mi Middly I O	See Si Siddly Si So
Strumming on the old banjo.	Strumming on the old banjo.	Strumming on the old banjo.

Ask the children to suggest another consonant sound to replace the /f/, (e.g., /l/, Lee Li Liddly I O, etc.). Start rocking or patting the steady beat, introduce the new lyrics by singing on the stating pitch of the song, and then sing with new lyrics.

Facilitation and Reflection

★ Which consonant sound did you like best for the song? Why?

★ In "Willaby Wallaby Woo," how was "woo" changed to rhyme with your first name? How would you change "woo" to rhyme with your last name?

Extensions

Preschool-Grade 2

★ As a transition in sending children to different tasks, sing

Willaby wallaby w<u>aul</u>, an elephant sat on <u>Paul.</u>
Willaby wallaby w<u>aris,</u> an elephant sat on <u>Taris.</u>
Lillaby lallaby <u>leric,</u> an elephant sat on <u>Eric.</u>
Lillaby lallaby <u>laleria,</u> an elephant sat on <u>Valeria.</u>

After you have used this transition, sing up to the third underline and ask the children to sing the child's name that rhymes with *waris* (or whatever works with the children's names in your class). (This shows that they know the rhyming word that rhymes with *waris*.)

K-Grade 2

★ When singing the songs, have the children generate a visual using construction paper and markers, concentrating on initial sounds. For example, when singing "Willaby Wallaby Woo," a child could make a big W to give a visual of the letter that makes the sound they are singing with.

★ Use the same process of listening to and responding with "same" or "different" for comparing words to identify if they are rhyming words or have the same vowel sounds, beginning blends, ending sounds, ending blends, prefixes, and suffixes.

11

EXPLORING MOUTH SOUNDS

Children explore the sounds their mouths can make and how their mouths make those sounds. Older children use these sounds to create new words.

Movement & Music Curriculum Concepts
- Exploring and identifying sounds
- Expressing creativity in movement
- Feeling and expressing steady beat
- Moving in nonlocomotor ways

Literacy Curriculum Concepts
- Aural discrimination
- Making sound/letter connections

MATERIALS

★ Chart paper or whiteboard
★ Markers or dry-erase markers
★ "Jungle Beat" on the enclosed CD
★ CD player
★ Small mirrors (Extensions)
★ Tissues (Extensions)

STEPS TO SUCCESS

Preschool–Grade 2

Step 1
Ask the children, working in their personal space, to explore ways to make sound using only their mouth. (This activity will take place all at once and can be noisy.) Have the children discover several sounds, focus in on their favorite, and find a way to move their body to represent the sound.

Step 2
Ask the children to share and copy their favorite sound and the movement they chose to represent it. After two children share, begin comparing and contrasting the sounds for length of sound and how it is produced (lips, tongue, etc.). Continue comparing and contrasting sounds with the other children. (As the children are producing their mouth sounds, they continue with the movement they chose.)

Step 3

Use the recording of "Jungle Beat" from the enclosed CD to help you learn the song, and see the sidebar on Learning New Songs for tips on introducing new songs. Sing the song to the children, replacing "Karissa" with the name of one of the children: "They took their mouth and they made [name of child]'s sound." Then have that child and the rest of the class make that child's sound several times before continuing the rest of the song.

Step 4

Ask for another volunteer to share his or her sound and have all copy. Stop the sound. Start the steady beat by patting quietly, and sing "Beat, beat, ready to sing" as is demonstrated on the enclosed CD. Sing the song again with that child's name and mouth sound. Sing as many verses as there are volunteers.

K-Grade 2

Step 5

Have the children put together two or more sounds to create new "words" (such as *click clack*). Older children can write these new words on chart paper or the whiteboard.

Grades 1-2

Step 6

Have children write a story about aliens, and include these new words as a part of the language spoken by the aliens (for instance, *Click clack, click clack, whoosh*).

Learning New Songs

Have the children start a movement in steady beat (e.g., quietly patting their legs). Synchronize the movement by using an anchor word for each beat (e.g., "Beat, beat, beat, beat"). While keeping steady beat, say, for example, "Beat, beat, beat, listen," and sing the melody on a neutral syllable, such as "bahm." Sing the melody several times on a neutral syllable, encouraging children to join in singing on a neutral syllable. Sing "Beat, beat, ready to sing" using the beginning pitch of the song (as demonstrated on the enclosed CD), and ask the children to join in, singing the first verse of the song at least four times.

Facilitation and Reflection

★ What was your favorite mouth sound? Why? How was it made?

★ Which movement do you think matched the sound the best? Why?

Extensions

Preschool-Grade 2

★ Get out a class set of small mirrors, and have the children look to see how each sound looks as they make their sounds. Discuss where in the mouth that sound is made (for instance, /s/ is air coming between the teeth, and /b/ is formed with the lips with the voice engaged).

★ Give each child a tissue, and ask the children to hold the top corners with each hand in front of their mouths. Encourage the children to make sounds to see which sounds "move" the tissue. Repeat with letter sounds (e.g., /p/ will move the tissue while /m/ will not).

★ Ask the children to put one of their hands gently on the front of their neck (demonstrate this for the children) while making letter sounds. Ask the children which ones they feel (such as /m/) and which ones they do not feel (such as /f/).

Jungle Beat

© V. Johnson 1987

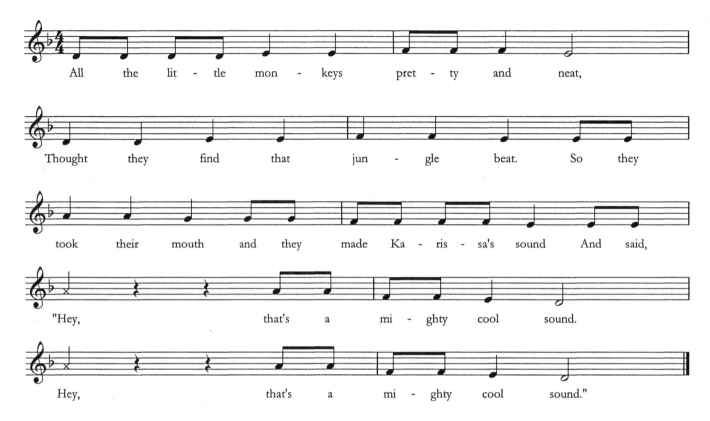

All the lit - tle mon - keys pret - ty and neat,

Thought they find that jun - gle beat. So they

took their mouth and they made Ka - ris - sa's sound And said,

"Hey, that's a mi - ghty cool sound.

Hey, that's a mi - ghty cool sound."

Verse 2

All the little monkeys pretty and neat,
Thought they find that jungle beat.
So they took their mouth and they made
Alejandro's sound
And said, "Hey, that's a mighty cool sound.
Hey, that's a mighty cool sound."

Verse 3

All the little monkeys pretty and neat,
Thought they find that jungle beat.
So they took their mouth and they made Ellie's sound
And said, "Hey, that's a mighty cool sound.
Hey, that's a mighty cool sound."

This child is joyous in sharing her movement and sound!

12

Exploring Positional Words Through Movement

Children explore different ways they can move and then use positional words to describe their movements and relationships to other children and objects.

Movement & Music Curriculum Concepts
- Expressing creativity in movement
- Moving in locomotor ways

Literacy Curriculum Concepts
- Expressing ideas in complete sentences
- Using positional words

Materials

★ *Rosie's Walk* by Pat Hutchins (Extensions)
★ Digital camera (Extensions)

Steps to Success

Preschool–Grade 2

Step 1

Have the children explore all the things in the room that they can walk around (e.g., tables, chairs, you). Ask "What did you walk around?" Have the children explore all the things in the room that they can go over. Ask "What did you go over?" Repeat this process with *under*. You can also do this activity when the children are on the playground outside.

K–Grade 2

Step 2

Have the children explore different ways they can walk in relation to a partner and tell their partner where they are walking in relation to him or her (e.g., "I am walking beside you").

Step 3

Have the children make a plan for one way to move in relation to their partner. Ask a volunteer to share how and where he or she moved in relation to his or her partner and then ask the other children to copy how the

volunteer moved. Continue with sharing and copying, making certain that the children explain the relationship (e.g., "I went *under* Masahiro").

FACILITATION AND REFLECTION

★ What were you able to go *under, around, beside,* and *through* on the playground or in the classroom?

★ How else could you go *around* the table? (Crawl, run, tiptoe, and so forth.)

★ What other places are you able to go *under, around, beside,* and *through?* For example: "At home I can crawl under my bed." (Notice how the sentence structure becomes more complex and the language is richer.)

The playground is a wonderful place for children to explore positional words.

EXTENSIONS

Preschool–Grade 2

★ Read *Rosie's Walk* by Pat Hutchins, and have the children retell the story through movement.

★ Support the children as they make a plan for an obstacle course. Ask each child to make a plan using one positional word, such as *between;* depending on the age of the child, you may need to help with the written directions. Have the children follow the directions through the obstacle course and recall as many positional moves they used as possible. Take photos of the children doing their positional moves and include the written directions. Put the photos into a class book that the children can read and reread and reenact the moves.

The children here have used an easel to explore under.

FAVORITE WORDS IN STEADY BEAT

Children use steady beat to say their favorite words and explore different ways of keeping steady beat.

Movement & Music Curriculum Concepts
- Feeling and expressing steady beat
- Moving in locomotor ways
- Moving in nonlocomotor ways

Literacy Curriculum Concepts
- Learning new words
- Recognizing the sounds that make up words

MATERIALS

★ None

STEPS TO SUCCESS

Preschool–Grade 2

Step 1
Ask children to think of and say their favorite word. For example, children may choose a dinosaur name, such as Allosaurus.

Step 2
Start the movement by quietly patting your legs with both hands. Encourage the children to join you in this movement, and then have the children take turns saying their favorite word. (All children should say their favorite word eight times.) Be sure that each child speaks the word naturally (not broken apart in syllables) and that everyone pats on the accented syllable of the word. For example, with the word Allo<u>sau</u>rus, the pat should be on the underlined syllable. All children should say the word eight times. Ask for another child's favorite word, and repeat the process each time.

Step 3
Have another child choose where to keep the steady beat, such as patting on the head, and repeat the process saying that child's favorite word. Be sure to remember to say the word eight times.

Step 4

Follow instructions in Steps 1–3, but only say the word four times instead of eight times.

Step 5

Have the children use words that they are using in science, for example, vol<u>ca</u>no, e<u>rup</u>tion, <u>la</u>va (the underline represents where the accent is for each word, which is where the pat will occur).

Step 6

Ask the children to work with a partner and find other ways to keep the steady beat (e.g., twist, rock) while they are saying their favorite words.

Patting on the body helps children feel the steady beat.

Grades 1-2

Step 7

Have the children sing their favorite words while keeping the steady beat by rocking or patting. Then have children stand up, step the beat, and say their favorite words. The favorite word is said each time one foot touches the floor.

Facilitation and Reflection

★ What was your favorite word today?

★ Why did you choose your word to say today?

★ What sounds are in your favorite word?

★ Where do you pat in your favorite word? Is it the beginning, middle, or end of the word?

Making Connections

Older students, after many times of experiencing this steady beat work, will be able to identify whether they touch down on the beginning, middle, or end of the word. The underlying steady beat allows them to have a feeling/hearing connection with the accented syllable of words.

The Four Seasons

Using Vivaldi's The Four Seasons *as inspiration, children represent the seasons through movement. They create a word bank about the seasons and use the word bank to write descriptive paragraphs.*

Movement & Music Curriculum Concepts

- Moving in locomotor ways
- Moving in nonlocomotor ways
- Responding to music

Literacy Curriculum Concepts

- Describing objects, events, and relations
- Understanding that the spoken word can be recorded as text
- Using descriptive language

Materials

★ A recording of Antonio Vivaldi's *The Four Seasons*

★ CD player

★ Chart paper or whiteboard

★ Markers or dry-erase markers

★ Paper for children to write on (Extensions)

★ Writing instruments (pencils, markers, crayons, etc.) (Extensions)

★ Digital camera (Extensions)

Steps to Success

K–Grade 2

Step 1

Ask the children to explore movements to represent the current season. For example, a child might think about the fall season and respond by moving in a fluttery way while moving arms toward the ground (representing leaves falling off a tree).

Step 2

Ask the children to make a plan of their favorite movement for the current season, and have them share their plan with a partner. The partner then copies the plan, and the two children do the movement together. Have the children switch roles.

Step 3

Encourage the children to describe their movements and what the movement represents from the current season. Compile a list of the children's descriptions and how their movements relate to the season on the chart paper or whiteboard.

Step 4

Have the children listen to one of the movements from Vivaldi's *The Four Seasons*. Although each season is represented musically with three separate sections in Vivaldi's entire piece, we recommend that you begin with the following movements of *The Four Seasons:*

- Spring — I Allegro
- Summer — III Presto
- Autumn — III Allegro
- Winter — II Largo

Have the children listen and move to the music for at least one minute before stopping the music, using your judgment of when you should stop each selection.

Step 5

Have the children try out their movement ideas from the compilation of children's descriptions now with the corresponding music (see Step 3).

Step 6

Replay selections from *The Four Seasons,* and have the children plan which movement ideas they can do to make it match the music. If they want to, the children can add additional movements to match the music.

Kindergarten students will not have had the experiences to do this activity until each season happens. This activity, therefore, can be repeated throughout the year as each season begins and can serve as a great recall of previous seasons to revisit and reread what the children had written from the past seasons.

Step 7

Encourage the children to brainstorm descriptive words and phrases for weather, climate, and seasonal variations, and write these phrases and words on chart paper or the whiteboard. Use this word bank to support the children as they write descriptive paragraphs about each season.

Facilitation and Reflection

★ What did you like about the fall (spring, summer, winter)?

★ How did you move to represent fall (spring, summer, winter)?

★ What influenced your choice of movements?

★ How did the music affect your movement plan?

★ What were some phrases and words that you heard from others that you had not considered?

Extensions

K-Grade 2

★ Use children's movement plans and sentences to make a class book about each season using digital pictures, drawings, and dictation or children's writing.

★ Use a word bank of descriptives to create cinquain poetry (see the glossary for a definition).

★ For another activity related to seasons, see Activity 44.

FROM SEED TO PLANT

Children listen to a story about how a seed becomes a plant and represent this sequence of events through movements.

Movement & Music Curriculum Concepts

- Expressing creativity in movement
- Moving in nonlocomotor ways

Literacy Curriculum Concepts

- Sequencing
- Writing in various ways: drawing, scribbling, and using letter-like forms, invented spelling, and conventional forms

MATERIALS

★ Book-making materials (paper, staplers, writing instruments)

★ "Seed to Plant" on the enclosed CD

★ CD player

★ A book on how a seed becomes a plant, such as *From Seed to Plant* by Gail Gibbons, *The Tiny Seed* by Eric Carle, *Jack's Garden* by Henry Cole, or *How a Seed Grows* by Helene J. Jordan

★ Digital camera (Optional)

STEPS TO SUCCESS

Preschool–Grade 2

Step 1

Tell the story of how a seed becomes a plant (listen to the story on the enclosed CD for an example). Alternatively, you can read the class a book about how a seed becomes a plant (see suggested books in the Materials section).

As they listen to the story, ask the children to represent the sequence of seed to plant through movement. For example, as you tell (or read) about how the seeds are small and tight in the cold ground, the children can make themselves small and tight as if they were seeds. Then, as you describe how the seed grows, the children move themselves as seeds growing from the earth.

Step 2

Have the children make illustrations of the sequence of events. Alternatively, take pictures of the children expressing the sequence of events through movement.

K-Grade 2

Step 3

Have the children write text to match the illustrations or pictures. Bind the pages to make a book, and use it for rereading the story.

Facilitation and Reflection

★ What did your body do to "grow"?

★ What can you say about the changes that take place in the sequence of seed to plant?

★ How did you show that through your movement?

★ What else goes through similar changes?

Extensions

Preschool-Grade 2

★ Use the steps in this activity with other life cycles such as life cycles of mammals, birds, reptiles, insects, amphibians, and human growth. Other good children's books that relate to this theme include *From Caterpillar to Butterfly* by Deborah Heiligman and *Tadpole to Frog* by Wendy Pfeffer.

★ See Activity 57 for an activity about the water cycle.

Having concrete experiences (in this case, representing the life cycle of a plant through movement) helps children understand complicated sequences.

16

GETTING IN, OUT, AND AROUND

Children make shapes with yarn, make plans on how to get in and around these shapes, and then use these movement plans with music.

Movement & Music Curriculum Concepts
- Describing movement
- Expressing creativity in movement
- Labeling movement
- Moving in locomotor ways

Literacy Curriculum Concepts
- Describing objects, events, and relations
- Using positional words

MATERIALS

★ 3-foot lengths of yarn

★ "Sally Go Round the Sun" on the enclosed CD

★ CD player

★ Paper for children to draw on (Extensions)

★ Writing instruments (pencils, markers, crayons, etc.) (Extensions)

STEPS TO SUCCESS

Preschool–Grade 2

Step 1

Ask the children to make a shape with their yarn on the floor that they can get into and out of. Encourage them to explore ways to go around their shape (e.g., gallop, walk backward, crawl), and ask them to share and copy their movement with the other children. Have the children describe their movement; for those children who do not have a word for their movement, supply a label. Let them know that when you say "Boom," they need a plan for how they will get into their shape, such as jumping into the shape.

Step 2

Have the children move around their shape, and ask a child to volunteer as the leader to say "Boom." Ask the children to make new plans for going around and getting into the shape.

Step 3

Have the children move around their shape while you sing or chant "Sally Go Round the Sun," ending with "Boom" at the end. At the end of the song, ask the children to make a plan for how they will go around their shape. Alternatively, give a label for how to go around the shape (e.g., hop, walk backwards, tiptoe, and so forth), and ask the children to show that they understand that label.

Step 4

Sing or chant the song replacing "Sally" with the children's names. When you sing or chant a child's name, the child does his or her movement around the shape while the rest of the class copies.

Facilitation and Reflection

★ What is your favorite way to go around your shape? To get into your shape? Why?

★ What does your body do when you are moving in your favorite way?

Extensions

K-Grade 2

★ Make a template of "Sally Go Round the Sun," and have the children write their name and movement. See the other verses for "Sally Go Round the Sun" for ideas.

★ Have the children put their yarn lengths together to make bigger shapes until everyone joins.

Sally Go Round the Sun

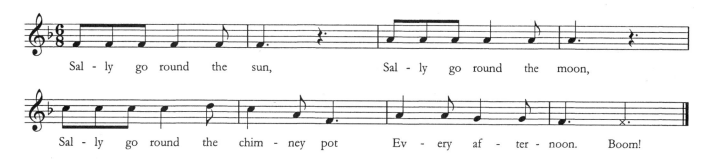

Verse 2
Sunjin go round the sun,
Sunjin go round the moon,
Sunjin go round the chimney pot
Every afternoon. Boom!

Verse 3
Dimitri go round the sun,
Dimitri go round the moon,
Dimitri go round the chimney pot
Every afternoon. Boom!

Verse 4
Manasi skip round the sun,
Manasi skip round the moon,
Manasi skip round the chimney pot
Every afternoon. Boom!

Verse 5
Jack jump round the sun,
Jack jump round the moon,
Jack jump round the chimney pot
Every afternoon. Boom!

Hello in Many Languages

Children explore different ways to say "Hello friends" through movement and in different languages.

Materials

★ "Hello Friends" on the enclosed CD

★ CD player

★ Chart paper or whiteboard (Extensions)

★ Markers or dry-erase markers (Extensions)

★ World map or globe (Extensions)

Steps to Success

Preschool–Grade 2

Step 1
Ask "How many ways do we know how to say hello?" Encourage the children to explore different ways of saying "hello," including ways without talking (e.g., waving).

Step 2
Say "Watch and copy," and begin patting the steady beat with both hands, remembering to use the rocking beat and not the marching beat. (The rocking beat is twice as long as the marching beat: One rock/pat equals two marches.) Begin the patting again, have the children copy, and then sing the melody of "Hello Friends" on a neutral syllable such as "bahm," encouraging the children to join in as they feel comfortable.

Step 3

Start the steady beat again, introduce the song using the starting pitch of the song, and sing the greeting song with the words "Hello friends." (This is demonstrated on the enclosed CD.) Sing the song several times, and encourage the children to chime in on the parts they remember.

Step 4

Ask the children, "In what other language can we sing this song?" (Their answers will depend on what languages are spoken in their homes.) Using their answers, start the steady beat movement; introduce the song by singing "Bahm, bahm, be ready now to sing" or "One, two, ready, sing"; and sing the song several times, encouraging the children to join in. If you know sign language (or know of someone who does), share with the children how to sign "Hello friends."

Step 5

Have the children ask their parents or grandparents if they know how to say "Hello friends" in another language, and encourage them to bring this information to class.

FACILITATION AND REFLECTION

★ Did each way to say "Hello friends" sound the same? Why not?

★ How are the alphabets/letters different or the same in other languages?

★ Which languages read from left to right, right to left, and/or bottom to top?

EXTENSIONS

K-Grade 2

★ Write "Hello friends" on chart paper or the whiteboard in the many languages that the children know or bring from home. Encourage the children to write the ones they know.

★ Have children locate on a world map or globe the location of each country represented in the song. Include this information in a class book. What is unique about each country?

Hello Friends

Verse 2 (Spanish)
Hola amigos hola. Hola amigos hola.
Hola amigos, Hola amigos,
Hola amigos hola, Hola.

Verse 3 (Japanese)
Konichiwa tomodachi.
Konichiwa tomodachi.
Konichiwa,
Konichiwa, Konichiwa tomodachi, Konichiwa.

Verse 4 (Hebrew)
Shalom chaver.
Shalom chaver.
Shalom chaver, Shalom chaver,
Shalom chaver shalom, Shalom.

18

HOW DO YOU MAKE THAT SOUND?

Using classroom instruments as well as improvised sound sources, children experiment with sounds of different durations and use movement to represent these sounds.

Movement & Music Curriculum Concepts
- Approximating sounds
- Exploring vocal sounds
- Playing simple musical instruments
- Sorting

Literacy Curriculum Concepts
- Reading graphs
- Manipulating sounds
- Strengthening mouth muscles for clear articulation

MATERIALS

★ Classroom music instruments and/or improvised sound sources

STEPS TO SUCCESS

Preschool–Grade 2

Step 1
Have available a variety of classroom music instruments and/or improvised sound sources such as kitchen implements, jars filled with different materials, and bubble wrap. Encourage the children to explore ways to make sounds with the instruments or the improvised sound sources.

Step 2
Ask the children to represent the sounds with movement that lasts as long as their sounds last. For example, bubble wrap has a short, popping sound; the child could make a quick move, such as jump. Each time the child jumps, the child would add a mouth-popping sound. An example of a longer duration of sound would be a child holding a pot lid by the knob (so the metal is suspended) and hitting the metal lid with a stick or mallet. The sound made by hitting the pot lid would last for a long time. The child would then hit the pot lid again, move for as long as the sound lasts, and add the sound of the pot lid. Have the children approximate their instrument's sound with their voices so that they feel the duration of the sound.

Step 3

Ask the children to volunteer their sounds, and have the rest of the children choose a movement to represent that sound and approximate the sound with their voices. Compare and contrast the duration of the different sounds by asking the children which sound lasted longer and which sound lasted only a short time.

K–Grade 2

Step 4

Help the children graph the sounds by their duration of sound, as shown in this example at the right.

Step 5

Ask the children to think of other places where they can find sounds to sort and chart (e.g., the recess bell, microwave oven signal, train whistle, car horn).

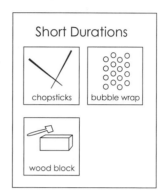

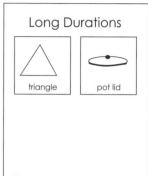

Step 6

Ask the children what letter sounds can be done in long duration (continuant)? (*l, m, n, o, s, z*) What letter sounds can be only be done in short duration (stopped)? (*b, c, d, g, h, j, t*)

Facilitation and Reflection

★ Which sound lasted the longest/shortest?

★ How did you show the longest/shortest sound?

★ Which sound was your favorite? Why?

★ What sounds could be made to have a short duration and a long duration?

★ What other ways could the duration of sounds be graphed?

Extensions

K–Grade 2

★ Graph letter sounds by their duration of sound.

★ Use long/short duration sounds and movement to embellish a story that children know. In the story "Three Billy Goats Gruff," an example of a short duration might be "Trip, trap, trip, trap" (say the words quickly for the short duration). An example of a long duration might be "Who's that trip trapping across my bridge?" (Exaggerate the length of the words as you read that line in the story.)

★ Have the children create a sound story using the instruments or sound sources as the sound effects and act out the story with the movement and sound. With older children, have them work in small groups and then share their stories with the other children. The children can categorize and graph the length of sound of the instruments or sound sources from longest to shortest in their story.

★ Ask the children to find items at home that have sounds of different duration.

19

The Human Chalk Board

Children draw shapes and letters in the air and create sounds that represent those shapes. Older children extend on this by drawing letters and words on each other's backs and on paper.

Movement & Music Curriculum Concepts
- Describing movement
- Exploring pathways
- Moving in nonlocomotor ways

Literacy Curriculum Concepts
- Writing in various ways: drawing, scribbling, and using letter-like forms, invented spelling, and conventional forms

Materials

★ Chalkboard, chart paper, or whiteboard
★ Chalk, markers, or dry-erase markers

Steps to Success

Preschool–Grade 2

Step 1
Ask the children to watch and copy, and then put your arms straight out in front with your palms together. Draw a shape or pathway in the air, and then ask the children to copy you. Encourage the children to explore making other shapes and pathways in the air and to describe the shapes or pathways that they make in the air.

Step 2
Ask for a volunteer who would be willing to let you draw on his or her back. With palms together so that you are using two hands, slowly draw a shape on the child's back allowing him or her to feel the shape. On the second time, have the child with palms together put his or her hands out in front so that when you draw again the child will draw the same shape in the air. The third time, both of you draw the same shape and the child adds any sound he or she wants. Repeat this step with other volunteers.

Step 3

Have children choose letters that they know, such as the first letter of their name. Support children as they explore writing letters they know in the air using both hands in front of them. Ask for a volunteer. First, draw the shape of the chosen letter on the child's back to have him or her feel the stroke. Next, have the child put his or her arms out in front and draw the shape as you draw the shape of letter again on the child's back. On the third time, ask the child to add a sound of his or her choice to the shape that you are drawing on the child's back while drawing the same shape out in front of him or her. Repeat this step with other volunteers as time permits.

K-Grade 2

Step 4

Have children find a partner and follow the process that is described in Step 2. Then ask the children to choose a letter and follow the process in Step 3.

Step 5

Have the children being "drawn" upon in Step 4 go to the board or chart paper, hold a marker or piece of chalk between the palms of their hands, and draw the letter that they explored in Step 4. (*Note:* For preschoolers, the chart paper must be on the wall, not on the desk or floor.)

Grade 2

Step 6

Have the children find a partner and draw three-letter words on the partner's back using the process in Step 3. The child being drawn on identifies the word.

Facilitation and Reflection

★ What shapes did you draw in the air?

★ How did you decide what shape you were going to draw?

★ Because you couldn't see the shape or letter, how did you know what the shape was?

Older children can work as partners to write and identify letters.

20

"I can..."

Children create and share a movement plan to represent something they can do independently and then use illustrations or words to represent their plan.

MATERIALS

★ Large sheets of paper

★ Writing instruments (pencils, markers, crayons, etc.)

★ Stapler or other book-binding materials

★ Digital camera (Optional)

STEPS TO SUCCESS

K–Grade 2

Step 1
Ask the children to explore movements that represent things they can do independently, such as read, play ball, or ride a bike. Ask them to make a movement plan to represent their favorite thing to do. Encourage them to share their movement plan with a partner or the whole group; their partner or the whole group copies and describes the movement plan.

Step 2
Have the children write what they had planned and shared by completing the following sentence: I can...

Step 3
Ask the children to illustrate and write their own plan as a page in a big class book. Alternatively, use a digital camera picture to take pictures of the children's plans and bind them into a class book.

FACILITATION AND REFLECTION

★ How did you decide what your plan to share would be?

★ What other plans had you considered?

EXTENSIONS

K-Grade 2

★ Have the children sing the text from the class book using random pitches and represent each page through movement as they read the book.

★ Help the children create other movement books using the following ideas as starters:

I like to…
I wish I could…
I would like to…
When I am at the beach (mountains, airport, museum, pool, concert, park, library), I always…
When I grow up I will…

Grades 1-2

★ Have small groups of children each choose a character from a story, such as "The Gingerbread Man," to act out and perform for the class. Then ask each child to pretend that he or she is the character and write about the character using one of the following sentence starters:

I can…
I live…
I want…
I move…
I know…
I wish I…
Next time I would…

★ Have children illustrate their sentences and create a class book.

Sentence starters help children use complete sentences to communicate their thoughts.

21

IDentifying Sounds to Retell a Story

Listening to the popular Peter and the Wolf, *children use movement to represent the story's characters and retell the story.*

Movement & Music Curriculum Concepts
- Exploring vocal sounds
- Moving to music
- Moving in locomotor ways
- Moving in nonlocomotor ways

Literacy Curriculum Concepts
- Comparing and contrasting
- Listening to stories and poems
- Retelling

MATERIALS

★ Recording of Prokofiev's *Peter and the Wolf*
★ CD player
★ Digital camera (Extensions)
★ Book-making materials (Extensions)

STEPS TO SUCCESS

Preschool–Grade 2

Step 1
Before listening to *Peter and the Wolf,* have the children explore ways that the characters (the child, cat, duck, wolf, grandfather, hunters, birds) might move and sound. Ask them to share and copy each other's ideas and compare and contrast their movements and sounds.

Giving a child the opportunity to lead while other children copy validates that child's ideas and builds confidence.

Step 2

Have the children listen to the excerpts and themes of *Peter and the Wolf*. Ask them to represent each of these characters with movement with the sound this time being the recorded music.

Step 3

Have the children retell the story through movement.

FACILITATION AND REFLECTION

★ How did you decide how your character would move and sound?

★ How did the music change your ideas?

★ How did the composer of *Peter and the Wolf* represent each character?

★ How did you know when that character returned to the story?

EXTENSIONS

Preschool-Grade 2

★ Listen to the story again either as a group or in a listening area.

★ Take pictures of the children acting out the story, have the children dictate what words should accompany the pictures, and make it into a big book that can be read (and reread).

★ Use another musical story and repeat the steps for this activity.

22

I'M Digging Like a Dog: Identifying Initial Consonants

After identifying initial consonant sounds, children choose words that begin with these sounds and plan movements that represent these words.

Movement & Music Curriculum Concepts
- Acting upon movement directions
- Describing movement
- Moving in locomotor ways
- Moving in nonlocomotor ways

Literacy Curriculum Concepts
- Identifying initial consonant sounds
- Using alliteration
- Using initial blends
- Using letters and names

Materials

★ Alphabet books

★ Picture dictionary such as *The Cat in the Hat Beginner Book Dictionary* by P. D. Eastman

Steps to Success

K–Grade 2

Step 1
Have the children browse through your classroom's collection of alphabet books and/or picture dictionaries to look for initial consonant sounds. Ask the children to choose an initial consonant sound, such as /d/. Have the children explore ways to move like things that start with that sound.

Step 2
Ask the children to make an individual plan of how they can move the way something that starts with that sound moves (e.g., dinosaur, dog, dancer, dump truck). Encourage them to share their plan with a partner or with the whole group. As the children travel from here to there, have them do so in their planned way.

Teacher's Tip

This activity can be used as a transition in moving to small groups, outdoors, lunch, and hand washing.

K-Grade 2

Step 3

Use the same process in Steps 1 and 2 for initial blends, such as /sh/ as in *ship* or *sheep*.

Grades 1–2

Step 4

Have the children choose verbs that begin with a chosen sound, such as *dancing, digging, dropping*. Then ask the children to choose adverbs to accompany the verbs (*dancing daintily, digging dangerously*). Ask them to mix them up (*dancing dangerously, digging daintily*) and to move in the various ways suggested.

FACILITATION AND REFLECTION

★ How did you make your plan?

★ Which other plans did you try that someone else shared?

★ Make a sound to go with your plan.

Having a selection of books that children can easily browse through encourages them to explore books on their own (and at their own pace).

23

INitial CoNSoNaNt SoUNDS: SaME oR DiFFERENT

Children first explore the concepts of same and different through movement and then listen to words that begin with same or different sounds.

Movement & Music Curriculum Concepts
- Describing movement
- Exploring and identifying sounds
- Moving in nonlocomotor ways

Literacy Curriculum Concepts
- Knowing a letter's sound or a sound's letter
- Identifying initial consonant sounds
- Recognizing the sounds that make up words

MaTERiaLS

★ Construction paper (Extensions)
★ Markers (Extensions)

STEPS To SUcCESS

Preschool–Grade 2

Step 1
Say "Watch and copy." Put both hands on your knees, and ask the children where your hands are (children will answer that they are on your knees). Ask "Are my hands both in the same place?" Model complete sentences to answer, such as "Yes, my hands are on my knees. They are both in the same place." Put both hands on your shoulders, and ask the children to copy what you do. Ask "Are my hands both in the same place on my body?" and have the children answer the question using complete sentences as you had modeled.

Step 2
Ask the children to explore other places they can put their hands so that they are on the same body part. Encourage them to use complete sentences as they say out loud where their hands are. (This part of the activity establishes the concept of *same.*)

TEaCHER'S TiP

Many young children do not know or cannot use *different* and are more comfortable and successful with *not the same* until their vocabulary has been developed.

Step 3

Say "Watch and copy." Place one hand on your shoulder and one hand on your nose. Ask the children to copy and encourage them to tell you where their hands are in a complete sentence (e.g., "One hand is on my shoulder and the other is on my nose").

Step 4

Ask the children to explore the many ways they can place their hands in two different places on their bodies. Have them use complete sentences to describe the placement of their hands. (This part of the activity establishes the concept of *different*.)

Step 5

Have the children recall and label some of the ways they showed *same* and *different*. For example, a child might put both hands on her feet and label this pose *same*. Then she might put one hand on her stomach and the other on her back and label it as *different*.

Step 6

Vocalize two sounds that are the same. Tell the children that they will hear two sounds. Ask them to repeat the sounds and determine if they are the same or different. If the two sounds are the same, ask them to respond by finding a place to put their hands like they did earlier to show *same*. If the sounds are *different*, ask them to respond by putting their hands in different places. Repeat the two sounds that are the same, with the children responding with *same* by showing with the placement of their hands. Repeat the sounds, and have the children repeat them also so the children can double-check their response.

Step 7

After modeling a few examples, ask for volunteers to provide the sounds for the rest of the class to listen to and respond with *same* or *different*. Encourage the children to use a wide variety of sounds that they can make with their mouth.

> **Making Connections**
>
> Vocal exploration with sounds provides children with purposeful opportunities to use different mouth shapes and tongue placement and also strengthens oral motor muscles, which is needed for clear articulation in speech.

K-Grade 2

Step 8

Working with a partner, have one child vocalize two sounds while the other listens, repeats the sounds, and responds as *same* or *different*. Encourage the children to talk about their responses and then switch roles.

Step 9

Say two words for the children to determine if they begin with the same sounds, and ask them to repeat the words and respond with the placement of their hands as *same* and *different*. Follow Steps 6–7 using sets of words.

Step 10

Working with partners or small groups, have the children take turns saying two words to determine if the words begin with the same sounds or different sounds and representing same of different with the placement of their hands.

FACILITATION AND REFLECTION

★ How do you figure out if sounds are the same or different?

★ How did you represent *same* or *different?*

24

MAKING LETTERS WITH YOUR BODY

Children use their bodies to make letters of the alphabet and then use other materials to represent alphabet letters.

Movement & Music Curriculum Concepts
- Describing movement
- Moving in nonloco-motor ways

Literacy Curriculum Concepts
- Knowing a letter's sound or a sound's letter
- Using letters and names
- Writing in various ways: drawing, scribbling, and using letter-like forms, invented spelling, and conventional forms

MATERIALS

★ An ABC book that shows different ways to make the letters of the alphabet (e.g., *Alphabet Movers* by Teresa Benzwie, *Alphabatics* by Suse MacDonald, *Alphabet Under Construction* by Denise Fleming, *Discovering Nature's Alphabet* by Krystina Castella and Brian Boyl, *Gone Wild: Endangered Animal Alphabet* by David McLimans)

★ 7-foot yarn lengths, modeling clay, or play dough

★ Digital camera

★ Train/racecar track lengths or blocks (Extensions)

★ Geoboards and rubber bands (Extensions)

★ Chart paper and writing instruments (Extensions)

STEPS TO SUCCESS

Preschool–Grade 2

Step 1
Have the children explore in their personal space stopped/static movements in which arms or legs are straight. Ask them to share, copy, and describe their statues. Then have them explore stopped movements in which arms or legs are bent. Ask them to share, copy, and describe these movements with the class.

Step 2

Have the children explore stopped movements in which arms, legs, or other body parts are curved, and ask them to share, copy, and describe their stopped movements.

Step 3

Share a selected ABC book (see the suggested titles under Materials). As children look at each page, pause so the children can decode and try to represent the way in which the picture depicts the letter of the alphabet. Talk about how the picture forms the letter.

Step 4

Ask the children to try to make the letter that starts their name with their body.

Step 5

Take digital pictures to make your own alphabet book of the children in their letter shapes.

Step 6

Have the children make a favorite letter with modeling clay, play dough, or the long yarn lengths.

K-Grade 2

Step 7

Have the children make lowercase as well as uppercase letters with their own body.

Step 8

Ask the children to work as partners and form letters together.

FaciliTaTioN aNd RefLecTioN

★ How did you decode the pictures of the book that was read in class?

★ Which one did you like to make and why?

★ Which letters were straight? Bent? Curved?

★ Which letters were easy to make? Difficult? Why?

EXTeNSioNS

Older children can work as partners to form letters.

Preschool-Grade 2

★ Have the children find what letters they can form on geoboards with rubber bands.

★ Have the children find what letters they can make with materials in the classroom such as lengths of train or racecar track, blocks, and so forth.

Grades 1-2

★ Have children work as partners to form initial blends (such as *tr*) and then write lots of words that start with that blend.

★ Have children work as partners to form ending blends (such as *st*) and write down lots of words that end with that blend.

25

MAKING MOVING TO MUSIC MEANINGFUL

Children explore ways to move and describe their movements. They move intuitively to instrumental music, describe how this music influenced their movements, and use these descriptions for writing activities.

Movement & Music Curriculum Concepts
- Expressing creativity in movement
- Moving in locomotor ways
- Moving in nonlocomotor ways
- Moving to music

Literacy Curriculum Concepts
- Expressing ideas in complete sentences
- Using descriptive language

MATERIALS

★ "Popcorn," "Hole in the Wall," and "The Sally Gardens" on the enclosed CD
★ Selections of other instrumental music
★ CD player
★ Chart paper or whiteboard
★ Markers or dry-erase markers
★ Thesaurus (Extensions)

STEPS TO SUCCESS

Preschool–Grade 2

Step 1
Ask the children to move in a bumpy way. The children explore bumpy ways to move, volunteers share their ways to move, and all copy volunteers' movements.

Step 2
Ask the children to describe how the movement was bumpy and model for them how to use complete sentences to answer your question. For example, a child might say "My body was jerky." Write the descriptive words on a word chart. Ask "What is another way we could move?" and

repeat the process, encouraging the children to answer in complete sentences. Have the children share their way of moving, and write the descriptive words on the word chart.

Step 3
Play the selection "Popcorn" first, and ask the children to move the way the music makes them feel. Then play the selection "Hole in the Wall," and tell the children to move the way the music makes them feel. Use about 15–30 seconds of each selection. Ask "How did the music make you want to move?"

Step 4
Write the answers to the question from Step 3 on a word chart. Repeat Steps 3 and 4 with many styles or kinds of instrumental music (music without words), such as "The Sally Gardens."

K-Grade 2

Step 5
Use the words on the chart to add descriptive words to a class story.

Facilitation and Reflection

★ How did you move differently to each musical selection?

★ Why did you choose the movement you used?

★ What can you say about the words on the word chart?

★ Describe and represent with movement the words on the word chart as a check for understanding new vocabulary.

Extensions

Grades 1-2

★ Have the children use the words on the chart to enhance a story that they are editing.

★ Create lists of synonyms and antonyms using the words from the word chart. Add to these lists with words from a thesaurus.

Children should explore moving intuitively to the music before being asked to describe it.

26

MOVE THAT SOUND

Children play instruments and then add movement and vocal sounds that approximate the instruments' sounds.

Movement & Music Curriculum Concepts
- Approximating sounds
- Exploring vocal sounds
- Moving in locomotor ways
- Playing simple musical instruments

Literacy Curriculum Concepts
- Knowing a letter's sound or a sound's letter
- Recognizing the sounds that make up words

MATERIALS

★ Instruments (such as rhythm sticks, tambourines, wood blocks, sand blocks, and bells)

★ Sound sources (such as plastic bottles with rice, beans, or gravel and kitchen gadgets)

★ Paper for children to write on (Extensions)

★ Writing instruments (pencils, markers, crayons, etc.) (Extensions)

STEPS TO SUCCESS

Preschool–Grade 2

Step 1
Have the children play instruments, and ask them to make a plan on how to move like one of the sounds. Then have them make a vocal sound that approximates the sound of one of the instruments.

Step 2
Ask a volunteer to share his or her instrument, movement, and approximation of the sound. Have the rest of the group copy the movement and approximation of the sound. Ask for other children to volunteer their ideas while the rest of the group copies.

Step 3

Ask the children to make a plan to put two or three of their favorite sounds together that they explored earlier, sequencing them together without space in between. For example, the sounds *sh, pop,* and *aah* would become *shpopaah.* Encourage them to share their sequence and copy each other's sound sequence.

FACILITATION AND REFLECTION

★ How did you move to your sound? Why?

★ What sound that you made was your favorite? Why?

★ What are the sounds you used? Are they found in a word that you know?

★ What new words can you make up with sounds that you like?

★ What did your mouth do to make your sound? What did your tongue do?

EXTENSIONS

Preschool-Grade 2

★ Have the children write their sounds and/or words. This could be devised letters or shapes, for example, *shpopaah* might look like ⌒⌒⌒\⎪⁄⌒⌒⌒ . These words may be made up or real.

These children are exploring sounds with instruments and making a plan on how to move like one of the sounds.

MOVEMENT SEQUENCES*

Children explore ways to use locomotor and nonlocomotor movement to put together a three-sequence movement plan.

MATERIALS

★ Paper for children to write on (Extensions)

★ Writing instruments (pencils, markers, crayons, etc.) (Extensions)

★ Digital camera (Extensions)

STEPS TO SUCCESS

> **Making Connections**
>
> SAY & DO means that children *say* the words that define their actions (SAY) and they *match the movement to the words* (DO).

Preschool–Grade 2

Step 1

Have the children explore and label movements they know using SAY & DO.

Step 2

Ask a volunteer to show a movement of his or her choice, such as shaking hands in front in a fast way. Encourage the rest of the children to copy, and then have the volunteer label the movement (shake). Have the rest of the children label the movement as they do it. Ask another volunteer to show a different movement (such as jumping). Encourage the rest of the children to copy, with the volunteer labeling the movement (jump). Then have the rest of the children label the movement as they do it. Have one more volunteer choose and show a final movement (such as rocking back and forth). Again, have the other children join in while the volunteer

---

*This activity is for children who have experience in the exploration of locomotor and nonlocomotor movements.

labels the movement, and then have the children say the label (rock) while doing it. Put these movements in the order that they were shown (shake, jump, rock), so it becomes a three-movement sequence that the class does as a group.

K-Grade 2

Step 3
Place the children in groups of three. Ask each child to choose a movement to share with the other two. Then ask them to decide which movement comes first, which is next, and which movement is last so that they have their three-movement sequence.

Step 4
Ask for volunteers to share and lead the whole group in their sequence. Compare and contrast the different group's sequences.

Facilitation and Reflection

★ What were some of the movements?

★ What was one of the sequence plans?

★ How did you make your plan for a three-movement sequence?

★ What else is designed in a three-sequence plan that has a first, next, and finally?

Extensions

K-Grade 2

★ Ask the children to work with a partner to make up a three-part sequence of events involving tasks (e.g., jump to the sandbox, skip to the climber, and walk backward to the slide). Have the children make up a story (first, next, finally) using their sequence of events and write it down. Ask them to illustrate the story or use a digital camera and take pictures of their sequence. What problems came up, and how were they solved?

★ Have children describe and retell the sequence of events in a known story and act out the sequence.

★ Ask the children what things they do in a special order (e.g., making a toasted cheese sandwich or getting ready for school). Does the order matter?

28

MOVING EMOTiONS

Children use movement to show emotions they have experienced, add sounds to their movements, and then use words to describe their movement/sound representation.

Movement & Music Curriculum Concepts
- Describing movement
- Exploring vocal sounds
- Moving in locomotor ways
- Moving in nonloco-motor ways

Literacy Curriculum Concepts
- Building vocabulary
- Using descriptive language

MATERiALS

★ Chart paper or whiteboard
★ Markers or dry-erase markers

STEPS TO SUCCESS

Preschool–Grade 2

Step 1

Have children start in their personal space. Start the activity by saying something like "I noticed that some of you came in sleepy today. Can you show me how you move when you are sleepy?" As children begin to move, encourage them to add vocal sounds to accompany their movement. When the children stop, ask "How did your body move when you were feeling sleepy?" Write their responses on chart paper or on the whiteboard. Ask "How did your voice sound when you were feeling sleepy?" Write their responses.

Step 2

Encourage the children to come up with other emotions that they sometimes feel. Ask the children to show a movement that represents that emotion and to add vocal representation. Write each emotion with descriptive words of what the body does and what the voice does to express each emotion. For example, the children may say that they made a fist and their hands were tight when they were mad or that their body was limp when they were tired. Write the words *tight* and *limp* on the chart paper or the whiteboard.

Step 3

Have the children write their responses to each new emotion they suggest. With the younger children, encourage them to write down the feeling words (e.g., *sad)* and have them say the word (e.g., *sad)* out loud so that they hear the letters that they will write to record the emotions. Do this after each emotion has been enacted.

When children have enough room to explore in their personal space, they can be anonymous and are comfortable expressing themselves.

Facilitation and Reflection

★ How did your body move to each emotion? How were your movements the same and/or different?

★ How did your voice sound for each emotion? How were your sounds the same and/or different?

★ Compare the vocabulary on the charts. What do you notice?

★ What do descriptive words add to stories?

Extensions

K-Grade 2

★ Use the charts to add descriptive words to stories that the children are writing and/or editing.

★ Have the children add to the words on the charts as they find descriptive words in stories that they read.

★ Graph the vocal representations of the emotions that the children share from highest sound to lowest sound.

NaMes iN STeaDy BeaT*

Children feel and express steady beat using the natural flow of speech and begin to find the accented syllables in words.

Movement & Music Curriculum Concepts
- Feeling and expressing steady beat
- Moving in locomotor ways
- Moving in nonlocomotor ways

Literacy Curriculum Concepts
- Using letters and names

MaTeRiaLs

★ None

STePs To SuCCess

Preschool-Grade 2

Step 1
Say to the children "Watch and copy," and begin the steady beat, patting quietly with both hands on the knees. Bring the class into synchronization by saying "Beat, beat, beat, beat."

Step 2
Ask a child to volunteer his or her name, and, as a class, say it eight times as it is **naturally** spoken with syllables connected, touching down on the accented syllable. Keep the steady beat movement silent so that the beat is felt and the name will be able to be heard. Have the rest of the class start the silent, steady beat while you add the anchor. For example, say "Let's say <u>An</u>na." (In this example, Anna is the anchor word.) Repeat this with several other children's names.

TeaCHeR's TiP
For steady beat movements in the upper body, use the **macrobeat**, which is half as fast as a comfortable marching or walking tempo.

---

*Adapted from Phyllis S. Weikart and Elizabeth B. Carlton, *85 Engaging Movement Activities* (Ypsilanti, MI: High/Scope Press, 2002).

Step 3

Have another volunteer choose a place on his or her body to keep the steady beat and say that child's name.

Here are examples of a few names and where the pat would occur in the name (underlined text):

A<u>nn</u>a, <u>A</u>nna, An<u>na</u>, <u>A</u>nna
Ale<u>ja</u>ndro, Ale<u>ja</u>ndro, Ale<u>ja</u>ndro, Ale<u>ja</u>ndro
E<u>li</u>zabeth, E<u>li</u>zabeth, E<u>li</u>zabeth, E<u>li</u>zabeth
Abuba<u>karry</u>, Abuba<u>karry</u>, Abuba<u>karry</u>, Abuba<u>karry</u>

FACILITATION AND REFLECTION

★ In what other ways can we use movement and speak our names? (Marching is an example.)

★ What other words could we say using steady beat?

EXTENSIONS

Preschool–Grade 2

★ Keep steady beat with other greeting songs or chants and with favorite words, remembering to start the beat first.

★ Have the children step in their personal space and speak names using locomotor movement, stepping down on the accented syllable of his or her name.

Grades 1–2

★ After the children have experience speaking their names using steady beat, ask "Where in your name do you touch or step down: beginning, middle, or end?"

Letting children choose where they want to pat the steady beat gives them ownership of the task.

30

The Nutcracker

Listening to "March of the Nutcracker," children intuitively respond to the music and use descriptive language to talk about and compare and contrast their movements.

Movement & Music Curriculum Concepts
- Expressing creativity in movement
- Moving in locomotor ways
- Moving in nonlocomotor ways
- Moving to music

Literacy Curriculum Concepts
- Learning new words
- Using descriptive language

Materials

★ Recording of "March of the Nutcracker" from Tchaikovsky's *The Nutcracker Ballet*

★ CD player

★ Paper for children to write on (Extensions)

★ Writing instruments (pencils, markers, crayons, etc.) (Extensions)

Steps to Success

Preschool–Grade 2

Step 1

Begin the recording of "March of the Nutcracker." Encourage children to move intuitively (without a plan), letting the music influence their movement. Ask for a volunteer to share his or her favorite movement and have the rest of the class copy. Ask the children to talk about the movement that was shared using descriptive language ("We were marching like a soldier," "My knees were up, high," "Our arms were swinging, but they were stiff and straight").

Teacher's Tip

When asking children to move intuitively, you, as the teacher, should *not* do the movement, as this causes the children to think they should move as you do.

Step 2

Ask another child to share what he or she did. Have the other children copy the movement and use descriptive language to say what they did. Now the children can try two of their classmates' ideas and compare and contrast those movements using descriptive language.

Facilitation and Reflection

★ What was your favorite march? Can you show it?

★ What words did you use to describe your march?

★ How did moving to "March of the Nutcracker" make you feel? What was it in the music that told you how to move?

★ What were some of the descriptive words and phrases that were used to describe your movements?

★ How do the descriptive words used to talk about your movements relate to what you heard in the music?

Extensions

Preschool–Grade 2

★ Have the children write cinquain poetry (see the glossary for a definition of cinquain poetry) to describe "March of the Nutcracker." (Preschool and kindergarten children can write the poem as a whole group.)

Grades 1–2

★ Have the children write about "March of the Nutcracker" and their movements using descriptive language.

★ Ask the children to suggest movement ideas for specific parts of "March of the Nutcracker."

★ Use "Trepak," "Arabian Dance," "Waltz of the Flowers," "Chinese Dance," and other parts of *The Nutcracker*. Follow the process of the children

   1. Intuitively responding to the music

   2. Sharing their movements

   3. Copying, describing, and comparing/contrasting their movements

   4. Facilitating and reflecting on the music and the movements

   5. Writing cinquain poems

★ Use scarves to explore and move intuitively to "Arabian Dance."

★ String the dances together with a simple narration written by the children, and perform an interpretation of *The Nutcracker* for parents or other classes.

31

ONE OF THESE THINGS IS NOT LIKE THE OTHERS

Children categorize several items as same or different and then create a movement plan to show how they categorized the items.

Movement & Music Curriculum Concepts
- Labeling movement
- Moving in locomotor ways
- Sorting

Literacy Curriculum Concepts
- Describing objects, events, and relations
- Sequencing

MATERIALS

★ Categorical items such as plastic or stuffed animals and like/different items (e.g., a box of tissues, pencil, stapler, book)

★ Paper for children to write on (Grades 1–2)

★ Writing instruments (pencils, markers, crayons, etc.) (Grades 1–2)

★ Digital camera (Grades 1–2)

★ Video camera (Optional)

STEPS TO SUCCESS

Preschool–Grade 2

Step 1
Ask "How are we all alike?" Then ask "How are we different?"

Step 2
Show three items that can be categorized in more than one way, such as a stuffed dog, stuffed turtle, and a plastic snake. Ask how they are alike. Then ask how are they different. Ask the children to represent the different movements of the animals. Discuss how these movements represent the differences.

K–Grade 2

Step 3
Put children in small groups, and give them three or four items to categorize (e.g., pencil, stapler, book, box of tissues).

Encourage them to discuss how these items are alike and different and the attributes and functions of the items.

Step 4

Have the children plan two movements to use (one to represent the items that belong together and one to represent the item that does not belong). Have them describe the items by listing attributes, functions, origins, and so forth, and decide which two or three items belong together and which one does not. Encourage them to explain their answers.

Step 5

Ask the children to create a movement plan that shows which items go together and which do not. For example, one group might plan to march for the items that go together and stomp for the items that do not belong. This group might have put the items in this order: pencil, stapler, book, box of tissues. The children could march, stomp, march, and march. Have the rest of the group copy, describe the plan, and then identify which items the group categorized as the same and which one was different. (In this movement plan, the children put all the products that originate from wood together; thus, the stapler is different.) Another group might choose to classify by location and put the pencil, stapler, and book together based on the location in the classroom. Those three items are readily available on the tables, but the tissue box is put next to the sink. Their movement plan might be to jump for the items that belong together and do a 360-degree turn in place for the item that does not fit. If the order was pencil, stapler, book, and box of tissues, then the movement plan would be jump, jump, jump, turn. Have the other groups copy the movement plan and try to decide how the group that shared classified the objects.

Grades 1–2

Step 6

Using Step 5, Grades 1–2 children can write how they classified their objects and how their movement plan represents their classification.

Step 7

Have the children plan their own four-item puzzle for others to process and pose movement solutions. Use a digital camera to capture the puzzles and movement plans to compile with written solutions as a class book or use a video camera to show the work of the children. Depending on the logical reasoning skills of the children, the puzzles can be very simple or quite complex. In one of our classes, a child took a picture of the sink, toilet, water fountain, and classroom door. When asked to represent this through a movement plan, the other children offered two solutions: Clap, clap, clap, jump, which was the first movement plan, represented that the first three items were water related but the fourth (the door) was not. The second movement puzzle (pat feet, pat feet, pat stomach, pat feet) was a bit harder to solve. The children's reasoning? The sink, toilet, and door were close to the floor but the water fountain was attached to the wall at a much higher level.

Facilitation and Reflection

★ How did you decide which item did not belong?

★ What were other ways to classify the items?

★ What do we find out when there is more than one way to classify or categorize?

32

OPPOSITES

Using their voices and their bodies, children represent words that are opposites. They listen to a song and then change the lyrics so that the lyrics contain pairs of opposites.

Movement & Music Curriculum Concepts
- Acting upon movement directions
- Distinguishing between high and low
- Moving in locomotor ways
- Moving in nonlocomotor ways

Literacy Curriculum Concepts
- Identifying synonyms and antonyms
- Rewriting a song

MATERIALS

★ "Opposites to the Tune of Looby Lu" on the enclosed CD

★ CD player

★ Chart paper or whiteboard (Extensions)

★ Markers or dry-erase markers (Extensions)

STEPS TO SUCCESS

Preschool–Grade 2

Step 1
Encourage the children to explore different ways to show high/low using their voice and body. Ask volunteers to share, encourage the other children to copy, and then describe and compare and contrast their movements and vocal sounds.

Step 2
Sing "Looby Lu" (see p. 81), and encourage children to join in. (See the sidebar for Learning New Songs — it is helpful to prepare children with the steady beat and the tonal center of the song before singing as a group.)

Have the children give ideas for others to follow for the first two lines of the second part of "Looby Lu":

> You put your hands and voice way up high,
> You put your hands and voice way down low.

These lyrics will change based on the children's plans for using pairs of opposites. Pause the song so that the children can do their movement and sound. For example, sing, as demonstrated on the enclosed CD, "You put your hands and voice way up high," pause, and allow time for the children to respond with the movement and a high voice. Then continue, singing "You put your hands and voice way down low." Pause again, and give children time to do the movement and to respond in a low voice.

K–Grade 2

Step 3

Ask the children to work with a partner to brainstorm and explore other pairs of opposites (e.g., quickly/slowly, in front of/in back of, apart/together) and ways to represent them using their voice and body.

FaciliTaTioN aNd RefleCTioN

★ What words were opposites? (*High* and *low* might be an example.)

★ Which opposites were your favorites? Why?

★ What opposites did you and your partner choose?

★ Where else do you find opposites?

★ How can we tell if pairs of words are really opposites?

Learning New Songs

Have the children start a movement in steady beat. Synchronize the movement by using an anchor word for each beat (e.g., "Beat, beat, beat"). While keeping steady beat, say, for example, "Beat, beat, beat, listen" and sing the melody on a neutral syllable such as "bahm." Sing the melody several times on a neutral syllable, encouraging children to join in singing on a neutral syllable. Sing "Beat, beat, ready to sing with me" using the beginning pitch of the song (as done on the enclosed CD), and ask the children to join in, singing the first verse of the song at least four times.

These children are exploring how to show "low" using their bodies.

EXTENSIONS

K-Grade 2

★ Follow Step 3 in this activity using different positions (e.g., near/far, closed/open, in front of/behind), verbs (e.g., run quickly/run slowly, jump high/jump low), and circumstances (e.g., you're cold/you're hot, you're big/you're small). Write on chart paper or the whiteboard the opposite words that the children used.

Grades 1-2

★ Use the words from the chart paper or the whiteboard to create a story, entitled "The Land of Opposites."

Older children can work in pairs to explore opposites, as shown by these two children.

Opposites to the Tune of Looby Lu

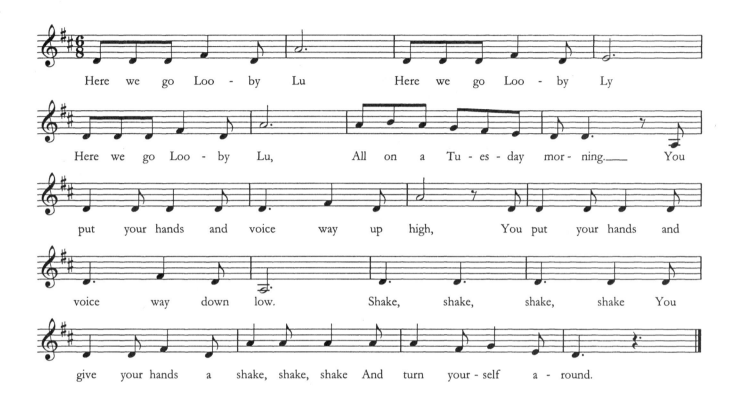

Here we go Loo - by Lu   Here we go Loo - by Ly
Here we go Loo - by Lu,   All on a Tu - es - day mor - ning.___ You
put   your hands   and   voice   way   up   high,   You put   your hands   and
voice   way   down   low.   Shake,   shake,   shake,   shake   You
give   your hands   a   shake, shake, shake   And   turn   your - self   a - round.

Verse 2

Here we go Looby Lu
Here we go Looby Ly
Here we go Looby Lu,
All on a Tuesday morning.
You put your hands way in close.
You put your hands way out far.
Shake, shake, shake, shake
You give your hands a shake, shake, shake
And turn yourself around.

Verse 3

Here we go Looby Lu
Here we go Looby Ly
Here we go Looby Lu,
All on a Tuesday morning.
You put your hands way out in front of you.
You put your hands behind you.
Shake, shake, shake, shake
You give your hands a shake, shake, shake
And turn yourself around.

Verse 4

Here we go Looby Lu
Here we go Looby Ly
Here we go Looby Lu,
All on a Tuesday morning.
You run very fast in place.
You run very slowly in place.
Shake, shake, shake, shake
You give your hands a shake, shake, shake
And turn yourself around.

Here we go Looby Lu
Here we go Looby Ly
Here we go Looby Lu,
All on a Tuesday morning.

33

"PAINTING" WITH AN IMAGINARY PAINTBRUSH

Children use an imaginary paintbrush to "paint" different pathways and letters in the air.

Movement & Music Curriculum Concepts
- Exploring pathways
- Moving in locomotor ways

Literacy Curriculum Concepts
- Using pathways to create letter shapes

MATERIALS

★ None

STEPS TO SUCCESS

Preschool-Grade 2

Step 1
Using both hands to hold an imaginary paintbrush, have the children explore drawing pathways in the air in front of them. Ask them to explore, plan, and share new ways to hold the paintbrush and to try each other's plans.

K-Grade 2

Step 2
Have children practice their spelling words with the imaginary paintbrush (with a partner or independently).

Making Connections

In this activity, children are exploring straight, zigzag, and curved pathways. Children begin to combine these pathways to make letters, numbers, and shapes with which they are familiar.

Facilitation and Reflection

★ How did you choose to hold your paintbrush?

★ Which ways were easier for you? Why?

★ How did you make the different positions work for you?

Extensions

K–Grade 2

★ Ask partners to share the same "paintbrush" (both holding on) and work together on words from a list of high-frequency words, sight words, environmental words, or a word wall. (Our children have also worked and moved together standing side by side to work on writing the words they know. They have also initiated working back to back with their partner, pretending to hold their imaginary paintbrush between them.)

These children are exploring pathways with their imaginary paintbrushes.

34

PEOPLE iN OUR TOWN*

Children feel and express steady beat while hearing and reciting a poem. They use movement and vocal sounds to express the poem's meaning and then substitute their own words into the poem.

Movement & Music Curriculum Concepts
- Distinguishing between high and low
- Exploring vocal sounds
- Feeling and expressing steady beat
- Moving in locomotor ways

Literacy Curriculum Concepts
- Making new verses
- Reciting poetry
- Story/poem innovation

MaTeRials

★ "People in Our Town" on the enclosed CD

★ CD player

★ Chart paper or whiteboard

★ Markers or dry-erase markers

★ Construction paper, glue, or digital camera (Extensions)

STeps To Success

K–Grade 2

Step 1

Ask a child to start walking, and have the rest of the group match the leader's tempo. Bring the group to synchronization by saying "Walk" every time the leader's foot touches the floor. Share the following poem, but leave out the sound at the end. (The poem is recorded on the enclosed CD.) The underlined words correspond with the marching beat:

> **People in Our Town**
> There are people in our town
> Going for a walk today. _____
> The wind is blowing so very hard
> It turns us the other way. _____ Ooooh!

---

*Adapted from Phyllis S. Weikart and Elizabeth B. Carlton, *85 Engaging Movement Activities* (Ypsilanti, MI: High/Scope Press, 2002).

Step 2

Ask the children what might happen if the wind blows very hard, and ask them to think about the sound it might make. As children volunteer sounds, have the class copy and add movement to represent the sounds.

Step 3

Speak the poem again, and include the sound at the end. (The sound in the poem moves from low-high-low on "Ooooooooooooooo.") Have the children show the direction of the sound of the wind with their arms (up and then down — like a siren). Then add the sound to the movement. Say the poem again, emphasizing the line: "It turns us the other way." Have the children add the sound of the wind and movement with their arms.

Step 4

Put Steps 1–3 together: Ask a volunteer to start the walk and bring the children to group synchronization in the walking beat set by the leader by saying "Walk, walk, walk, walk." Add the poem, encouraging children to join you in reciting it, and have the children turn around as they make the low-high-low vocal sound while moving their arms up and down. Repeat several times.

Step 5

Have the children decide what kind of people or animals live in "our town" and substitute that name for "people" in the poem. Ask them to represent how those people or animals would walk, and try each new idea first before saying the poem. Listen to this example on the CD:

> There are horses in our town
> Going for a gallop today. _____
> The wind is blowing so very hard
> It turns them the other way. _____ Neighhh!

Step 6

Write (or have the children write) the names of people or animals on chart paper or a whiteboard.

Facilitation and Reflection

★ What happens when the wind blows hard?

★ What if the wind were blowing lightly? How would this change our poem?

★ How did your movement change when you changed characters in the poem (e.g., baby crawled, old man limped, skater skated)?

★ What was your favorite character? Why? How did you move?

Extensions

K-Grade 2

Make a template of the poem leaving out the word "people" so the children can write in their favorite character. Have them glue their poem onto construction paper and add illustrations. Put these into a class book that the children can read. Alternatively, take a digital picture of the children moving as if they were their favorite character, and use this in place of the hand-drawn illustration.

35

POLAR, BEAR, POLAR, BEAR, WHAT DO YOU HEAR?

Children explore moving and making sounds like animals they know, listen to Polar Bear, Polar Bear, What Do You Hear? *and then approximate the sounds and movements of the animals in that story.*

Movement & Music Curriculum Concepts
- Describing movement
- Exploring and identifying sounds
- Moving in locomotor ways

Literacy Curriculum Concepts
- Describing objects, events, and relations
- Story/poem innovation
- Using descriptive language

MATERIALS

★ *Polar Bear, Polar Bear, What Do You Hear?* by Bill Martin and Eric Carle

★ Chart paper or whiteboard

★ Markers or dry-erase markers

★ Paper for children to write on (Extensions)

★ Writing instruments (pencils, markers, crayons, etc.) (Extensions)

STEPS TO SUCCESS

Preschool–Grade 2

Step 1
Ask the children to explore moving like animals that they know. As they are moving, have them add the sound that the animal makes.

Step 2
Have the children make a plan of one animal's movement they can share. Ask a volunteer to show his or her movement representation, and encourage the other children to join in to copy the leader. Ask the children to describe how the animal moved and what else they noticed about what the leader was showing. The leader then says the name of the animal that he or she had in mind. Ask the children to explore the sounds made by that animal. Then, as they are moving as if they were that animal, encourage them to add sounds.

Step 3

Have the children talk about and describe the sounds of the animal and approximate and compare and contrast the different sounds made by the same animal (e.g., high/low, long/short duration, quiet/loud). In what situations might each sound be made by this animal?

Step 4

Read *Polar Bear, Polar Bear, What Do You Hear?* As each sound and animal is mentioned, pause to provide opportunities for the children to explore the movements and approximate the sounds described in the text.

K-Grade 2

Step 5

Create a word bank on chart paper or the whiteboard of descriptive words about the movement and sounds (e.g., long, low, high, short, whistling, grumbly, growling, trumpeting, scratching, thudding, soft, light, tinkling) that could be used in children's writing.

Facilitation and Reflection

★ What did you notice about the animal sounds? How did you make them?

★ How were they different for the same animal?

★ What did your mouth do to make the differences?

★ Why were there different sounds for the same animal?

★ How did the movement change as the sound changed?

Extensions

Preschool-Grade 2

★ With the children, explore movements and sounds of machines, quality of character voices, job sites, and so forth.

★ Write descriptions about sounds (for preschool children, write the words on chart paper or the whiteboard; older children can write their words on separate pieces of paper and then share with the class). Use these descriptive words for writing.

K-Grade 2

★ Create a class book like *Polar Bear, Polar Bear* using the children's favorite animals.

36

Positional Words With Beanbag Sequences

Children use beanbags to explore positional words and create a two-movement sequence by placing beanbags on different parts of their body.

Materials

★ Beanbags — enough for two for each child

★ "The Beanbag Song" on the enclosed CD

★ CD player

★ Chart paper or whiteboard

★ Markers or dry-erase markers

★ Book-making materials (Extensions)

★ Digital camera (Extensions)

Steps To Success

Preschool–Grade 2

Step 1

Distribute the beanbags, making sure that children have a beanbag for each hand. (It is easier for young children to do the same thing with both sides of their body.) Encourage the children to explore where they can put beanbags on their body. Ask volunteers to share where they put the beanbags on their body while the other children copy. Then ask volunteers to describe where their beanbags are in relation to their body (e.g., "My beanbags are <u>out in front</u> of me," or "My beanbags are <u>on my feet</u>"). Encourage them to use complete sentences. Write (or have the children write) these sentences on chart paper or the whiteboard.

Step 2

Sing "The Beanbag Song" (you can use the enclosed CD to learn the song), and encourage the children to join in. See the sidebar for Learning New Songs — it is helpful to prepare children with the steady beat and the tonal center of the song before singing as a group.

Step 3

Using the sentences the children initiated in Step 1, sing the song again, changing the third phrase to rhyme with where the beanbag was (see the verses for the song for ideas).

Step 4

Recall two places that the children suggested, and build a two-movement sequence such as "shoulders, stomach." As children recall that shoulders was one of the places suggested, have them pat their shoulders and then add the label "shoulder" as they pat their shoulders (SAY & DO).

Ask the children to recall another place that they had initiated, such as the stomach. After the children begin patting their stomach, have them add the label "stomach" as they continue the movement. Challenge the children to try two places in succession, such as patting their shoulder and patting their stomach. (It is important that children have an opportunity to try, on their own, saying the label as they are doing the movement.) After trying two places in succession, have a volunteer start the movement (e.g., one pat on shoulder, one pat on stomach). Encourage the rest of the children to join in and then lead them in labeling the movement (say "Shoulder, stomach" several times) while doing it (SAY & DO). Sing "The Beanbag Song" again, as a class, this time replacing the lyrics with "Put your beanbag on your shoulder, on your stomach."

> SAY & DO means that children *say* the words that define their actions (SAY) and *they match the movement to the words* (DO).

Learning New Songs

Have the children start a movement in steady beat (in this activity, they can use their beanbags to keep the steady beat). Synchronize the movement by using an anchor word for each beat (e.g., "Beat, beat, beat, beat"). While keeping steady beat, say "Beat, beat, beat, and listen," and sing the melody on a neutral syllable such as "bahm." Sing the melody several times on a neutral syllable, encouraging children to join in singing on a neutral syllable. Have a child choose the position of the beanbag (e.g., feet), and have him or her start the steady beat. Sing "Bahm bahm, bahm bahm, ready sing" on the beginning pitch of the song (as modeled on the CD), and sing the first verse of the song at least four times, encouraging the children to join in as they feel comfortable.

K-Grade 2

Step 5

With a partner, have the children teach each other their sequences (using SAY & DO) and put them together to create a four-movement sequence.

Step 6

Ask pairs to perform their four-movement sequences for the rest of the group while you lead the class in singing "The Beanbag Song" with the corresponding lyrics to the movements performed.

Facilitation and Reflection

★ What was your favorite position of beanbag? Why?

★ What were the positions of your beanbag (e.g., on, over, under, around, and so forth)?

★ Where were the places that you used for your sequence?

EXTENSIONS

Help children create a class book with their verses to "The Beanbag Song." They can illustrate, or use a digital camera, to record their actions.

While a volunteer shares where she is putting her beanbags, the rest of the children copy the leader's movement.

The Beanbag Song
(Put Your Finger in the Air)

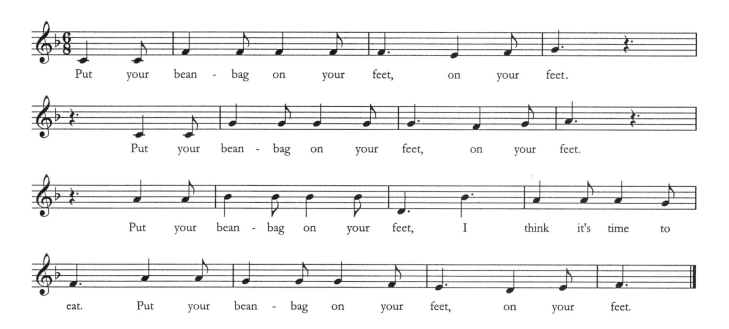

Put your bean - bag on your feet, on your feet.

Put your bean - bag on your feet, on your feet.

Put your bean - bag on your feet, I think it's time to

eat. Put your bean - bag on your feet, on your feet.

Verse 2

Put your beanbag on your knees, on your knees.
Put your beanbag on your knees, on your knees.
Put your beanbag on your knees, be careful not to sneeze.
Put your beanbag on your knees, on your knees.

Verse 3

Pat your hands on your chin, on your chin.
Pat your hands on your chin, on your chin.
Pat your hands on your chin and try not to grin.
Pat your hands on your chin, on your chin.

Verse 4

Pat your hands on your chest, on your chest.
Pat your hands on your chest, on your chest.
Pat your hands on your chest, then give them just a rest.
Pat your hands on your chest, on your chest.

37

PRACTICING VISUAL TRACKING

Children use visual tracking to copy each other's movements.

Movement & Music Curriculum Concepts
- Moving in nonloco-motor ways

Literacy Curriculum Concepts
- Visual tracking

MATERIALS

★ Balls (a variety of sizes and types such as playground rubber balls, tennis balls, and so forth) (Extensions)

★ Beanbags (Extensions)

★ Stuffed toys (Extensions)

STEPS TO SUCCESS

Preschool-Grade 2

Step 1

Have the children in their personal space face you. Say "Watch and copy," and make a sequence of movements. (The easiest movement for children to copy in the upper body is both sides of the body doing the same thing at the same time; for more information about the movement core, see p. 3.) For example, put both hands on your knees, pause so the children match your movement, and then put your hands quickly to the shoulders and then pause. Still moving symmetrically but now moving slowly, move your hands continuously from your knees to your shoulders. (When the movement is slow and continuous, the children copying the leader must rely on visual tracking to follow the movement.)

Making Connections

Children must have practice in visual tracking in order to read. The eye movement for reading is to follow the text from left to right with a sweep back to the left side of a page.

Step 2

Have the children make a plan for two places on their body that they could touch. Ask for a volunteer to lead the "watch and copy," and remind them to either get there fast and pause or go slowly between two places. Have several children lead.

Facilitation and Reflection

★ What two places did you choose?

★ Which way was easiest to follow, the "fast" way or the "slow" way? Why?

★ Where else do you have to track the movement of an object?

Extensions

Preschool–Grade 2

★ Give each child a ball. Ask them to bounce and catch or toss and catch the ball, tracking the movements with their eyes. This can be extended with older children by having them work with a partner. Ask them to share their strategies for tracking the ball in order to catch it. How did the strategies change when they are working with a partner?

K–Grade 2

★ Have children choose a partner, and have them lead each other in static or dynamic moves, beginning with symmetrical moves.

★ Give each child a beanbag for each hand. Have the children work with a partner and track and match each other's movement.

★ Give each child one beanbag to hold with both hands. Give verbal directions (but do not do the action) such as "Put your beanbag on one knee." Pause, and then say "Put your beanbag on one shoulder" so that children will opportunities to cross the midline. This can also be done as "watch and copy" where you demonstrate by putting the beanbag on one shoulder and the children copy the action.

★ Give each child a stuffed toy, and ask a volunteer to move his or her toy in different positions (high, low, over, under, in front of, in back of) while the other children match. Then have them try this with partners.

> **Crossing the midline** is the ability to move one hand, foot, or eye into the space of the other hand, foot, or eye. For example, patting your left shoulder with your right hand, crossing your ankles, or reading left to right.

38

Reality and Fantasy: How can We Tell The Difference?

Children explore the differences between reality and fantasy through movement and then create their own reality and fantasy stories.

Movement & Music Curriculum Concepts
- Describing movement
- Moving in locomotor ways

Literacy Curriculum Concepts
- Distinguishing between reality and fantasy
- Expressing ideas in complete sentences
- Listening to stories and poems
- Making up stories and rhymes

Materials

★ *I Know a Rhino* by Charles Fuge (Extensions)

Steps To Success

Preschool–Grade 2

Step 1
Ask the children to choose a way to move that reflects something they do every day (e.g., walking, skipping, or running). Have them share and copy each other's movements and then describe the movements. Explain to them that this kind of movement is reality (for younger children, use the term *real*) — these are ways that they really move in everyday situations.

Step 2
Ask the children to choose an animal and move as if they were that animal. Have them share and copy each other's movements and then describe the movements. Explain to them that this type of movement is fantasy (for younger children, use the term *not real*) — these are ways they can pretend to move.

K-Grade 2

Step 3

Have the children make a plan for how they are going to move in a way that is reality (real), such as moving like a soccer player on the field, or fantasy (not real), such as moving like a robot. Have them share, copy, describe the movement, and label the movement as reality (real) or fantasy (not real).

Grades 1-2

Step 4

Sing a "Once upon a time" story (e.g., a once-upon-a-time story about baseball), and ask a child to volunteer a part of the story. The child would plan whether his or her part of the story will be reality (real) or fantasy (not real). For example, a child might start a story based on reality in this way: "Once upon a time there was a boy named Brandon, and he liked to play baseball." Have all the children pause to represent the sentence with movement. Ask "Is this real?" (Their answer would be "Yes.") Ask another child to continue the story (e.g., "He was good at catching"), and have all the children represent that part with a movement. Ask "Is this real?" (Their answer, again, would be "Yes.") Encourage the children to use complete sentences in their story. Ask another child to continue (e.g., this child might say, "Brandon plays for the Yankees"), and represent this statement with movement. Ask "Is this real?" The answer for this question, would be, of course, "No" (fantasy), because Brandon is too young.

FACILITATION AND REFLECTION

★ How did you know if your movement was reality (real) or fantasy (not real)?

★ How do you know if a story is reality (real) or not fantasy (not real)?

EXTENSIONS

Preschool-Grade 2

★ As a class, write a group story that is reality or fantasy.

★ Do this movement activity around Halloween, and have the children choose a character that they might represent (a ghost, zombie, ballerina, baseball player) and decide whether that character is reality or fantasy. Which characters are real and which are not real?

K-Grade 2

★ Have the children sort classroom books into fantasy or reality.

★ Share with the class *I Know a Rhino* by Charles Fuge, a story in which a preschooler's fantasy play turns out to be reality.

39

RECALLING a FAMILIAR STORY

Children find ways to represent the events of a story with movement. Volunteers share their ideas, and the other children copy.

Movement & Music Curriculum Concepts
- Exploring the singing voice
- Expressing creativity in movement
- Moving in locomotor ways

Literacy Curriculum Concepts
- Listening to stories and poems
- Retelling

MATERIALS

★ Stories such as "The Little Red Hen," "The Three Bears," or poems that have a very clear sequence of events

STEPS TO SUCCESS

Preschool-Grade 2

Step 1
After reading your selected story, show again the story's illustrations, and ask the children to make their own plan of how they will use movement and sound to represent each event of the story. For example, in "The Three Bears," each character has its own voice and movement. Papa Bear's voice is low in pitch, and the children would probably show large movements and a low voice to represent him.

Step 2
Have the children retell the story by adding sound to the movement to represent the events in the story. On cue of a volunteer conductor, ask children to retell the story with their selected movement while using their singing voice to express their ideas in complete sentences. The conductor will give the group a signal to stop. Have all the children

TEACHER'S TIP

Using a child conductor highlights the concepts of start and stop, but, more important, provides the children with the safety net of knowing all children will be singing at the same time and no one will end up singing solo.

continue moving and singing (and maybe repeating what they've already sung) until the conductor gives the stop signal.

Facilitation and Reflection

★ What movement did you use to represent each part of the story?

★ How did your voice help you to represent the parts?

★ How did your voice change for each of the characters?

★ How will this help you to read other stories that have different characters, such as "The Little Red Hen"?

★ What other stories do you like to tell/read whose characters have different voices?

Extensions

Preschool-Grade 2

★ Use other familiar stories from the content areas or genre such as fairy tales, poetry, and rhymes such as "The Three Billy Goats Gruff," "Henny Penny," and "Hey Diddle Diddle." Repeat the process of movement and voice in Steps 1–2.

★ Use your singing voice in any situation where you would use your speaking voice (e.g., at greeting time or planning time or when you are giving directions or asking questions). Encourage children to use their singing voice in these situations as well.

As the teacher and child are looking at the illustrations, the child is making a plan on how he is going to move and the sound he is going to use.

REPRESENTING WORDS WITH MOVEMENT

Children explore different ways to represent a movement concept from a selected piece of literature.

Movement & Music Curriculum Concepts
- Describing movement
- Moving in locomotor ways

Literacy Curriculum Concepts
- Listening to stories and poems
- Relating pictures and text to real life

MATERIALS

★ *Max* by Rachel Isadora, or other literature selections that include movement concepts (see the list of movement books at the end of the book for suggestions)

★ Video clips of ballet performances and baseball games (Extensions)

★ Paper for children to write on (Extensions)

★ Writing instruments (pencils, markers, crayons, etc.) (Extensions)

STEPS TO SUCCESS

Preschool-Grade 2

Step 1
Introduce selected literature, and explore with the children the key movements described in the story. For example, in *Max*, by Rachel Isadora, children can explore various ways that baseball players and ballet dancers move. Encourage children to share, copy, compare and contrast, and describe the different movements of baseball players and ballet dancers.

Step 2
Read short sections of the story, pausing to provide opportunities for the children to interpret, represent, and experience different ways of movement that are described in the story. Have the children share with partners or the whole group, copy, describe, and compare and contrast the movements.

Step 3

Read the next part of the story, strategically pausing to provide opportunities for exploration and problem solving of how to represent each movement.

FACILITATION AND REFLECTION

★ What were some movements that you did (or other children showed you), and how did they fit in the story?

★ In planning your movement to represent different events in the story, what were some of the problem-solving strategies that you used? (Some children may share that they had to be careful about the available space around them for safety reasons.)

★ Compare and contrast movements for playing baseball and for performing ballet.

EXTENSIONS

Grades 1-2

★ View clips of ballet performances and baseball games, and have the children compare and contrast the movements in these clips. They can also compare the movements in these clips to other skills.

★ Ask the children to brainstorm and write about what it takes to excel at any sport or any skill. Have them write goals for themselves and devise their own plan on how they can work toward accomplishing those goals.

★ Encourage the children to bring other books or short pieces of literature to life through this process. See the list of movement books for more selections.

This child has chosen to be a ballet dancer.

41

RhyMiNG WORDS WiTh "The ANTS GO MARChiNG"

Children move while singing "The Ants Go Marching" and make their own rhyming verses to the song.

Movement & Music Curriculum Concepts
- Describing movement
- Feeling and expressing steady beat
- Moving in locomotor ways
- Singing songs

Literacy Curriculum Concepts
- Rewriting a song
- Rhyming

MATERIALS

★ "The Ants Go Marching" on the enclosed CD

★ CD player

★ Writing instruments (pencils, markers, crayons, etc.)

★ Paper for children to write on

STEPS TO SUCCESS

K–Grade 2

Step 1

Have the children explore different ways that they can march by themselves, and then ask them to share and copy each other's ideas. Have a volunteer be the leader, and have all the children join the leader, matching her timing and movement.

Step 2

Ask the children to plan to use one of their movement ideas. Have them start their movement, and bring the group into synchronization by singing "Beat, beat, beat, and listen" using the pitch that starts the melody. Sing the first verse of the song on a neutral syllable, such as "bahm" (as is done on the enclosed CD), and encourage the children to join in singing as they feel comfortable.

Sing "Bahm bahm, bahm bahm, ready now to sing" using the beginning pitch of the song (as demonstrated on the enclosed CD), repeating the first verse several times so that the children feel comfortable. (Not all children will be able to sing and move at the same time; some children need opportunities to move and listen. As they become more familiar with the melody and lyrics, they will begin to join in when they can.)

TEACHER'S TIP

Using the first pitch of the song prepares the children to start the song singing together with the same starting pitch.

Step 3

Repeat the song again, but this time ask the children to create a new line that rhymes with "one by one."

> The ants go marching one by one / The little one stops
> to _____

Have the children sing the song with the new rhyme and the movement that represents the rhyme. (See verse 2 on p. 103 for an example.)

FACILITATION AND REFLECTION

★ How did you come up with new words to rhyme with "one"?

★ What was one of your favorite rhymes? Why?

★ What was one of your favorite ways of marching? Why?

These children are having lots of fun moving to "The Ants Go Marching."

EXTENSIONS

K-Grade 2

★ Have the children find ways to travel two by two, sing the song replacing "one by one" with "two by two," and find words that rhyme with two (see verses 3 and 4 of "The Ants Go Marching").

★ Continue and have the children move in groups of three, four, and so forth, knowing that the group will not divide evenly.

★ Have children work in small groups to make up their own rhyming verses for the song (e.g., one stopped to have some fun, two stopped to paint the door blue, and so forth). Make a class book of their rhyming verses.

These two girls decided to travel this way "two by two"!

The Ants Go Marching
(When Johnny Comes Marching Home)

Patrick Gilmore

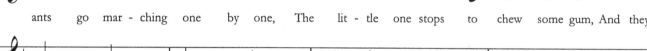

The ants go mar - ching one by one hur - rah, hur - rah, The

ants go mar - ching one by one hur - rah, hur - rah, The

ants go mar - ching one by one, The lit - tle one stops to chew some gum, And they

all go mar - ching down to the ground, To get

out of the rain... Boom, boom, boom, boom.

Verse 2

The ants go marching one by one hurrah, hurrah,
The ants go marching one by one hurrah, hurrah,
The ants go marching one by one,
The little one stops to have some fun,
And they all go marching down to the ground,
To get out of the rain....Boom, boom, boom,
boom.

Verse 3

The ants go marching two by two hurrah, hurrah,
The ants go marching two by two hurrah, hurrah,
The ants go marching two by two,
The little one stops to tie his shoe,
And they all go marching down to the ground,
To get out of the rain....Boom, boom, boom,
boom.

Verse 4

The ants go marching two by two hurrah, hurrah,
The ants go marching two by two hurrah, hurrah,
The ants go marching two by two,
The little one stops and hops like a kangaroo,
And they all go marching down to the ground,
To get out of the rain....Boom, boom, boom,
boom.

42

Sentence Punctuation Through Movement

Children represent with movement what happens at the beginning and ending of a sentence (e.g., capital letter, period).

Movement & Music Curriculum Concepts
- Moving in locomotor ways
- Moving in nonlocomotor ways

Literacy Curriculum Concepts
- Expressing ideas in complete sentences
- Using punctuation
- Writing in various ways: drawing, scribbling, and using letter-like forms, invented spelling, and conventional forms

Materials

★ Paper for children to write on

★ Writing instruments (pencils, markers, crayons, etc.)

Steps to Success

K–Grade 2

Step 1

Ask each child to create a movement plan to represent the beginning and ending punctuation of a short sentence of his or her choice. Take, for example, the sentence, "We like ice cream." A child might plan to spin around one time to represent the capital letter "W" to begin the sentence and jump to end the sentence with a period.

Step 2

Ask a volunteer to share his or her sentence, and help the children keep the steady beat as they chime in on the volunteer's sentence as it is repeated four times. Ask the volunteer to share his or her movement plan, and then have the children join in on the volunteer's movement plan as they say the sentence. Ask for additional volunteers to share their sentences and movement plans as time allows.

Teacher's Tip

Begin the steady beat first by patting silently and saying "Beat, beat, beat, and speak." Use a steady beat that is a comfortable rocking beat (half as fast as a comfortable marching or walking tempo). Encourage the children to join in with patting to the steady beat before the volunteer shares his or her sentence.

Step 3

Have the children write down their sentence using a capital letter to begin the sentence and ending punctuation.

FACILITATION AND REFLECTION

★ Why did you choose your movement for the beginning of the sentence?

★ Why did you choose your movement for the punctuation at the end of the sentence?

EXTENSIONS

K–Grade 2

★ Create opportunities to use "!" or "?"

★ Encourage children to work together to create several related sentences and sequence them in a logical order to create a paragraph. Have them recite their paragraph with their planned movements for punctuation. (Younger children may need adult help to write out their sentences with the punctuation.)

SING A SONG ABOUT PUNCTUATION*

Using a familiar tune, children create movements to represent different punctuation marks and then sing a song about the punctuation marks.

Movement & Music Curriculum Concepts

- Expressing creativity in movement
- Feeling and expressing steady beat
- Moving in locomotor ways
- Moving in nonlocomotor ways
- Singing songs

Literacy Curriculum Concepts

- Learning punctuation terms
- Sequencing
- Using punctuation

MATERIALS

★ "Ending Punctuation" on the enclosed CD
★ CD player
★ Chart paper or whiteboard
★ Markers or dry-erase markers

STEPS TO SUCCESS

K-Grade 2

Step 1

Start the steady beat by lightly patting your hands on your legs, and encourage children to join in keeping the steady beat with you. While keeping steady beat, introduce "Ending Punctuation" as demonstrated on the enclosed CD (e.g., say "Beat, beat, beat, listen," and sing the song on a neutral syllable such as "bahm"). Sing the phrases in "Ending Puncuation" one at a time, pausing after each phrase. Encourage the children to finish the phrases with the appropriate ending punctuation.

Step 2

Start the steady beat again by quietly patting your legs with both hands. Encourage the children to join you in this movement. Prepare the children

---

*This activity is most appropriate for kindergartners when they are in the second half of the school year.

to start the song (e.g., sing "Bahm bahm, bahm bahm, ready, sing with me" using the song's beginning pitch [as demonstrated on the enclosed CD]) and, as a class, sing the lyrics with the blanks filled in.

Step 3

Ask the children to make up a new movement to represent *period* (e.g., a single stomp). Have the children practice their movement plan for *period* and repeat the movement with the word (SAY & DO).

Step 4

Ask the children to make up a new movement to represent *question mark* (e.g., shrugging their shoulders to indicate "Huh?"). Have the children practice their movement plan for *question mark* and repeat the movement with the word (SAY & DO).

Step 5

Ask the children to make up a new movement to represent *exclamation point,* for example, a jump. Have the children practice their movement plan for *exclamation point* and repeat the movement with the word (SAY & DO).

Step 6

In this step, add the movements with the words that represent the movements (SAY & DO) to the phrases of the song. First, synchronize the stomp by using SAY & DO ("Stomp, stomp, stomp, stomp"), and have children join you in this steady beat movement. Then begin singing the first line of the song while the children stomp to the steady beat:

<u>If</u> it's a <u>state</u>ment <u>and</u> you <u>know</u> it, <u>use</u> a <u>peri</u>od._____ _____

Note: Movement happens on underlined syllables.

Sing the phrase several times encouraging children to join in. Stop singing and moving. Synchronize the shrug by using SAY & DO ("Shrug, shrug, shrug, shrug"), and have the children join you in this steady beat movement. Then begin singing this second line while the children shrug their shoulders to the steady beat:

> SAY & DO means that children *say* the words that define their actions (SAY) and *they match the movement to the words* (DO).

<u>If</u> it's a <u>ques</u>tion and you <u>know</u> it, use a <u>ques</u>tion mark._____

Sing the phrase several times, encouraging children to join in. Stop singing and moving. Synchronize the jump by using SAY & DO ("Jump, jump, jump, jump"), and have the children join in. Then begin singing these last two lines of the song while the children jump to the steady beat:

<u>If</u> you're ex<u>cit</u>ed <u>and</u> you <u>know</u> it, <u>let</u> your <u>punc</u>tua<u>tion</u> <u>show</u> it:
<u>If</u> you're ex<u>cit</u>ed <u>and</u> you <u>know</u> it, <u>use</u> an <u>excla</u>mation <u>point.</u>

When the children have done this several times, try it without stopping in between phrases.

Step 7

Have the children practice their movement for period four times followed by their movement for question mark four times. Have them say the appropriate word (either "Period" or "Question mark") while moving. For example, the children perform four stomps and then four shrugs at a rocking tempo and label their movements "Period, period, period, period, question mark, question mark, question mark, question mark."

Step 8

Have the children practice their movement for exclamation point eight times, saying "Exclamation point" for each jump.

Step 9

Do Step 7 immediately followed by Step 8. Have the children SAY the punctuation terms while they DO the movement.

FACILITATION AND REFLECTION

★ What do you know about punctuation marks?

★ How do they help you when reading and writing?

By lightly patting their hands on their legs, these children feel the steady beat while singing "Ending Puncuation."

Ending Punctuation
(If You're Happy and You Know It)

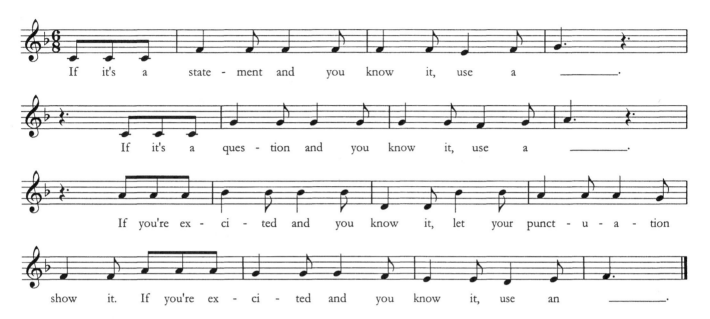

If it's a state - ment and you know it, use a _____.

If it's a ques - tion and you know it, use a _____.

If you're ex - ci - ted and you know it, let your punct - u - a - tion show it. If you're ex - ci - ted and you know it, use an _____.

44

SINGING ABOUT THE SEASONS

Children choose movements to represent seasonal happenings and then use their movements to write new verses to a familiar tune.

Movement & Music Curriculum Concepts
- Describing movement
- Moving in locomotor ways
- Moving in nonlocomotor ways

Literacy Curriculum Concepts
- Rewriting a song
- Using descriptive language

MATERIALS

★ Chart paper or whiteboard

★ Markers or dry-erase markers

★ "Raking All the Leaves" on the enclosed CD

★ CD player

★ *Fall Is Here! I Love It!* by Elaine W. Good (Extensions)

★ "Road to the Isles" on the enclosed CD or a recording of Vivaldi's *The Four Seasons* (Extensions)

STEPS TO SUCCESS

Preschool-Grade 2

Step 1

Have the children plan movements to represent current season happenings (e.g., children might show how to make leaves move in the wind). Encourage them to share their movement with the group; the other children copy and then describe their classmates' movements. Write children's ideas, movements, and descriptive words on chart paper or the whiteboard.

Learning New Songs

Have the children start a movement in steady beat (e.g., quietly patting their legs). Sychronize the movement by using an anchor word for each beat (e.g., "Beat, beat, beat, beat"). While keeping steady beat, say, for example "Beat, beat, beat, listen" and sing the melody several times on a neutral syllable, encouraging the children to join in singing on a neutral syllable. Sing "Beat, beat, ready to sing" using the beginning pitch of the song (as demonstrated on the enclosed CD), and ask the children to join in singing the first verse of the song several times.

Step 2

Sing "Raking All the Leaves" to the children, and encourage the children to join you in singing the song. See the sidebar for Learning New Songs for tips on introducing new songs.

Step 3

Have the children use their movements, ideas, and descriptive words to create new verses to "Raking All the Leaves."

Step 4

As a class, sing and act out new verses as suggested by the children with planned movements to match.

K-Grade 2

Step 5

Support children as they write and illustrate their new verses.

Facilitation and Reflection

★ How did you decide on movements and events to represent the current season?

★ What was your process to rewrite a verse for "Raking All the Leaves"?

★ How did you plan your movement to match the verses?

Extensions

K-Grade 2

★ Read together *Fall Is Here! I Love It!* by Elaine W. Good. There is a predictable phrase that occurs throughout the book. Have the children plan how many times they will repeat the phrase each time it occurs using steady beat.

★ Use "Road to the Isles" or a recording of Vivaldi's *The Four Seasons* to explore and plan movements for each season. For additional experience with the seasons, see Activity 14.

Children's excitement and natural enthusiasm about the changing seasons can be incorporated into singing and movement activities.

Raking All the Leaves

(Paw Paw Patch)

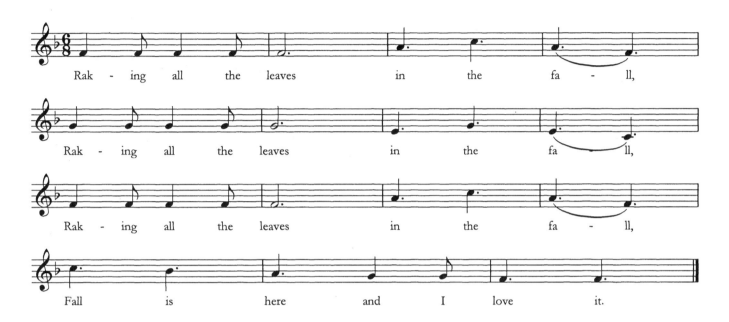

Rak - ing all the leaves in the fa - ll,

Rak - ing all the leaves in the fa - ll,

Rak - ing all the leaves in the fa - ll,

Fall is here and I love it.

Verse 2

Making a snowball in the winter,
Making a snowball in the winter,
Making a snowball in the winter,
Winter is here and I love it!

Verse 3

Planting seeds in the springtime,
Planting seeds in the springtime,
Planting seeds in the springtime,
Spring is here and I love it!

Verse 4

Going swimming in the summer,
Going swimming in the summer,
Going swimming in the summer,
Summer is here and I love it!

SINGING AND MOVING WITH MY STUFFED ANIMAL

Children move around their classroom and describe the daily routine by singing to their stuffed animals.

Movement & Music Curriculum Concepts
- Moving in locomotor ways
- Singing songs

Literacy Curriculum Concepts
- Describing objects, events, and relations

MATERIALS

★ Stuffed animals (children can bring their favorite stuffed animal from home)

STEPS TO SUCCESS

Preschool–Grade 2

Step 1
Ask the children to welcome their stuffed animals and help them feel comfortable by singing the greeting song such as "The More We Get Together" or "Good Morning" with steady beat.

Step 2
Have the children sing about the daily routine to their stuffed animal.

Step 3
Ask the children to give their stuffed animal a tour of the room and sing about what activities are done in each area. Encourage them to help the animals move in the ways that they move in each area.

Singing Familiar Songs Together

To sing the greeting song with steady beat, start the steady beat by quietly patting your legs with both hands. Encourage the children to join you in the movement; sing, for example, "Beat, beat, beat, and sing" on the first pitch or note of the song and begin singing the greeting song.

Facilitation and Reflection

★ What do you think your stuffed animal liked best in the room?

★ Where do you think your stuffed animal will choose to go during choice time?

Extensions

Preschool–Grade 2

★ Take a singing tour around the school or playground.

★ Have the children make a plan for taking their stuffed animal to do the things that they do in their favorite place on the playground. Have their animal do the movement they do when they go there.

Grades 1–2

★ Have the children create a story where their stuffed animal is the main character.

This girl is singing about the daily routine to her stuffed animal friends while taking a tour of the classroom.

STATUE CLONES*

Children explore statue shapes, use descriptive language to talk about each other's statue shapes, and use music to move around statue shapes.

Movement & Music Curriculum Concepts
- Moving to music
- Recognizing attributes of shapes

Literacy Curriculum Concepts
- Attending to details
- Describing objects, events, and relations
- Using descriptive language
- Visual awareness

MATERIALS

★ Recording of "Cherkessiya" or "Soldier's Joy" on the enclosed CD
★ CD player
★ Paper for children to write on (Extensions)
★ Writing instruments (pencils, markers, crayons, etc.) (Extensions)

STEPS TO SUCCESS

Preschool-Grade 2

Step 1
Ask the children to explore different statue shapes, and have all copy several children who volunteer to demonstrate their shapes. Ask the children to describe the statues (e.g., "What can you tell Victor about his statue?").

As each new statue is presented, copied, and described, have the children compare and contrast (e.g., "How was Victor's statue different or the same as Ellie's?"). Encourage them to pay attention to detail.

---

*Adapted from Phyllis S. Weikart and Elizabeth B. Carlton, *85 Engaging Movement Activities* (Ypsilanti, MI: High/Scope Press, 2002).

Step 2

Ask a volunteer to share his or her statue shape. Have the children form a circle with the volunteer in the center of the circle. Play either "Cherkessiya" or "Soldier's Joy" from the enclosed CD, and ask the children to move in the circle around the "statue." (By walking around the statue, the children are looking at the front, back, and sides of the "statue.") When the music stops, ask everybody to copy the statue in the center and talk about the statue using as much descriptive language as possible.

Step 3

Have the children find a partner, with one child being the statue and the other child being the traveler. Play the music again, and the "traveler" moves around the room. When you stop the music, the travelers return to their partners and copy their partner's statue. Encourage the travelers to describe their partner's statue in detail. The partners then change roles.

Grades 1-2

Step 4

Have the children keep one part of the statue moving to the steady beat of the music — even after the music has stopped (e.g., they might keep the beat by swinging one arm to the beat).

Step 5

Have the children make a statue that mirrors their partner's statue.

Facilitation and Reflection

★ Show us one of the statues that you liked. Why did you like it?

★ What made a statue easy to copy? Difficult to copy?

★ What was your favorite statue? Why? Can you remake that statue now? How did you remember how to make it?

Extensions

Preschool-Grade 2

★ See Activity 24 for an activity in which children use their bodies to make letters.

Grades 1-2

★ Have children draw the statues, title them, and write a story about them.

★ Ask the children to work with a partner. Each child chooses a letter, either uppercase or lowercase, and then describes his or letter in as much detail as possible as in this example: "The B has a straight line and curved lines like a 1 and a 3 combined. It takes up two lines on my paper. It would take both of us to form this letter as a statue on the floor." After each child has shared, have the children contrast the two letters. Ask for volunteers to share their statue of one or both of the letters with the class.

Steady Beat Stories

Children learn how to keep a steady beat and listen to a story that has an underlying steady beat.

Materials

★ Literature that has an underlying steady beat (see the list of movement books at the end of the book for examples)

★ "The Old Lady Who Swallowed the Fly" and "The Gingerbread Man" on the enclosed CD

★ CD player

★ *The Little Old Lady Who Was Not Afraid of Anything* by Linda Williams (Extensions)

Steps to Success

Preschool–Grade 2

Step 1

Ask the children to plan a way to keep a silent steady beat, such as rocking or patting their knees. Anchor the beat into synchronization by using an anchor word. For example, say "Beat, beat, beat, and speak." Begin the story (e.g., a version of the popular "The Old Lady Who Swallowed the Fly" or "The Gingerbread Man") while everyone continues to keep the steady beat. Have the children continue keeping the silent steady beat as they listen to you read a short part of the text using a natural flow of speech (not in a sing-song voice) layered on top of the steady beat. (Listen to the examples of "The Old Lady Who Swallowed the Fly" or "The Gingerbread Man" on the enclosed CD.)

Step 2

Ask the children to find a new way to keep the steady beat. Anchor the beat again, and continue with the next piece of the story (four to eight lines).

Facilitation and Reflection

★ What did you notice about the flow of the words?

★ How did keeping the steady beat help you listen to the text?

Extensions

Preschool-Grade 2

★ See the list of movement books at the end of this book for other examples of literature that has an underlying beat, and repeat the steps in this activity with other selections.

★ Read to the children *The Little Old Lady Who Was Not Afraid of Anything* by Linda Williams, a story where a little old lady encounters different things in the middle of the path. In this story, the shoes make a sound: "Clomp, clomp." Have the children act out how the shoes would clomp, and add the language, "Clomp, clomp, clomp, clomp, clomp...." Have the children say "Clomp" each time they take a step. This Extension gives children the opportunity to work in their own timing and with one-to-one correspondence (one word matching each movement in *repetition*, not only twice, as is in the text).

Making Connections

Some pieces of literature in their entirety do not continue with a steady beat yet have wonderful opportunities for children to feel and express a steady beat on a short recurring phrase. For example, "The Gingerbread Man" does not have an underlying pulse throughout the text, but the recurring phrase of "Run, run, as fast as you can. You can't catch me, I'm the gingerbread man!" is an opportunity for children to keep a steady beat as they chime in on this recurring phrase (listen to the sample story on the CD). Another example would be the recurring phrase in the book *Jump, Frog, Jump* by Robert Kalan. In the text, it is written only once, but the children can choose how many times to repeat the phrase as they keep the steady beat: Jump, frog, jump. / Jump, frog, jump./

Excerpt From "The Old Lady Who Swallowed the Fly"

There was an old lady who swallowed a fly,
I don't know why she swallowed a fly.
Perhaps she'll die.

There was an old lady who swallowed a spider,
That wiggled and jiggled and tickled inside her.
She swallowed the spider to catch the fly,
But I don't know why she swallowed a fly.
Perhaps she'll die.

Excerpt From "The Gingerbread Man"

Run, run as fast as you can
You can't catch me
I'm the Gingerbread Man.

48

Steady Beat Warm-Up Chart

Children make and chart a movement plan to the two sections of "Yankee Doodle." Using SAY & DO, children read and move through the charted movements with steady beat.

Movement & Music Curriculum Concepts
- Feeling and expressing steady beat
- Moving in locomotor ways
- Moving in nonlocomotor ways
- Moving in sequences to a common beat

Literacy Curriculum Concepts
- Reading in various ways: reading storybooks, signs and symbols, and one's own writing
- Writing in various ways: drawing, scribbling, and using letter-like forms, invented spelling, and conventional forms

Materials

★ "Yankee Doodle" on the enclosed CD

★ Other instrumental selections, such as "Soldier's Joy," "Joe Clark Mixer," and "Cherkessiya" (see the enclosed CD)

★ CD player

★ Chart paper or whiteboard

★ Markers or dry-erase markers

★ Digital camera (Extensions)

Steps to Success

K-Grade 2

Step 1

Ask the children to explore a variety of ways they can march in place. Some will try high or very small steps, steps with their legs wide apart, or steps with their toes pointing in or out. Encourage the children to share their ways of marching, copy each other's marching, and describe and label the movements. Each time a child shares his or her march, the rest of the class joins in and then adds the label "March, march, march, march" (SAY & DO).

Step 2

Sing the first verse (Section A) of "Yankee Doodle," without the words, on a neutral syllable, such as "bah."

Step 3

Help the children plan marching movements for the first section (Section A) of "Yankee Doodle." After they have a plan, have children do the marching movements and label the movement using SAY & DO. For example, children may march on their heels and say "Heel" each time one of their heels touches the floor. Write the children's movement plan on chart paper or the whiteboard (see the Simple Plan for Leading Music on p. 123). Make writing down the movements as interactive as possible, with children coming up with the labels for movements and supporting them as they write on the chart paper or whiteboard. Help children read and move through the charted movements for Section A.

> SAY & DO means that the children *say* the words that define their actions (SAY) and they *match the movement to the words* (DO).

Step 4

Sing the second verse (Section B) of "Yankee Doodle," without the words, on a neutral syllable, such as "bah."

Step 5

Ask the children to explore what they can do with their arms or hands to the second part of "Yankee Doodle" (Section B). Ask volunteers to share their movements with the group, copy each other's movements (using the SAY & DO process), and label and describe. It is easier for children if their movement is on the body (such as pat or pound). As each child shares his or her movement, bring the class to the steady beat by labeling the movement (such as "Pat, pat, pat, pat").

Step 6

Have the children make a movement plan for their hands and arms for Section B and then SAY & DO. Write the children's movement plan as you did in Step 3. Help children read and move through the charted movements for Section B.

Step 7

Practice the transitions from one section to the next using SAY & DO. When the plan and chart are complete, try all of the parts and then add the music. Begin moving after the introduction.

FACILITATION AND REFLECTION

★ What was your favorite way to march? Can you show it?

★ What was your favorite movement with your hands or arms?

★ How did you choose the variations for marching and for using your arms and hands?

★ How did you know when to change your movements?

(Please turn the page.)

EXTENSIONS

K–Grade 2

★ Make a similar chart with other musical selections (e.g., "Soldier's Joy," "Joe Clark Mixer," and "Cherkessiya").

Grades 1–2

★ Use a digital camera to take pictures of the children in position (e.g., hands on head or feet far apart). Put these pictures on the chart.

★ Have the children write a plan with a partner and then teach their plan to another pair of children.

★ Using other musical selections, continue with planning more AABB sections for the number of times that the music repeats:

  • "Soldier's Joy" has 7 AABB sections.
  • "Joe Clark Mixer" has 6 AABB sections.

Simple Plan for Leading to Music

Introduction: 8 beats   **Musical Form AB (6 times)**   "Yankee Doodle"

A section is locomotor movement.   *B section is nonlocomotor movement.*

1. A *March*   ⌐⌐   B *Pat head*

2. A *March*   ⌐⌐   B *Pat head*

3. A *March toes in*   ⌐⌐   B *Pat legs*

4. A *March toes in*   ⌐⌐   B *Pat legs*

5. A *March on heels*   ⌐⌐   B *Pat shoulders*

6. A *March on heels*   ⌐⌐   B *Pat shoulders*

SYNONYMS AND ANTONYMS

Children share their movement ideas and explore words that represent their movements. Then children share opposite movements and explore words that represent those opposite movements.

Movement & Music Curriculum Concepts
- Acting upon movement directions
- Describing movement
- Labeling movement
- Moving in nonloco-motor ways

Literacy Curriculum Concepts
- Describing objects, events, and relations
- Identifying synonyms and antonyms

MATERIALS

★ CD player (Extensions)

★ "Yankee Doodle" and "The Sally Gardens" on the enclosed CD (Extensions)

★ Chart paper or whiteboard

★ Markers or dry-erase markers

STEPS TO SUCCESS

K-Grade 2

Step 1
Have the children explore different ways to move.

Step 2
Ask a volunteer to share his or her movement. Everyone copies the volunteer's movement. Ask "How would you describe this movement?" For instance, a child may demonstrate a punching motion, which other children describe using words such as *punch, jab, poke, stab,* or *thrust.* Write the movement and the words given by the children on chart paper or the whiteboard. Ask for other volunteers to show their movements, and repeat the process. Introduce and explore the concept of *synonyms.*

Step 3

Ask another volunteer to show a movement on the chart or whiteboard but this time ask the rest of the class to show an opposite movement. For instance, the volunteer may demonstrate up by lifting her arms above her head and the other children would demonstrate the opposite direction (putting their arms down). Ask the children to describe their opposite movements. Write the words on the chart paper or the whiteboard to describe the opposite movement (in this example, it may be *low* or *down*). Introduce and explore the concept of *antonyms*. Ask for other volunteers to repeat this process, and write down each set of opposites on the chart paper or blackboard.

Facilitation and Reflection

★ What was your favorite movement? Why?

★ How many words can you use to describe your movement?

★ What do you now know about synonyms and antonyms?

★ What were your favorites? Why?

Extensions

Grades 1-2

★ Use the words on the chart paper or whiteboard for writing activities. For example, children could begin their story with the writing prompt: "Once Upon a Time in the Land of Opposites…"

★ Encourage the children to use the list of synonyms as a thesaurus to add more interesting words in their written stories.

★ Introduce an action word, such as *shake*. Try out synonyms appropriate to use with *shake*, and perform the synonyms to musical selections such as "Yankee Doodle" and "The Sally Gardens." Try the same process with antonyms.

TRACKiNG iN SEQUENCES

Children create sequences of movements and use steady beat to track and "read" these movement sequences.

Movement & Music Curriculum Concepts
- Feeling and expressing steady beat
- Moving in nonloco-motor ways
- Moving in sequences

Literacy Curriculum Concepts
- Sequencing
- Tracking visually left to right

MATERiALS

★ Attribute blocks, wooden beads, and laces (Extensions)

★ "Sauerländer Quadrille" on the enclosed CD (Extensions)

★ CD player (Extensions)

★ Digital camera (Extensions)

STEPS TO SUCCESS

Preschool–Grade 2

Step 1
Have the children explore some places on their body where they can pat both hands at the same time to feel steady beat.

Step 2
Ask for a volunteer to show where he or she patted. Have all the children join the leader, adding the label of the movement after the child has begun to pat (e.g., "Head, head, head, head"). Have another volunteer repeat the process. Recall the first child's and then the second child's movement.

Step 3
Have the first two volunteers come to the front and face the class. Recall the first child's and the second child's movement. SAY & DO with the class as they keep steady beat ("Head, head, head, head," "Chin, chin, chin, chin"). Repeat this process with two more children coming up to the front and sharing where they patted ("Feet, feet, feet, feet," "Stomach, stomach, stomach, stomach").

Step 4

As a class, recall the first two movements and make a pattern with labels ("Head, chin, head, chin, head, chin, head, chin"). Then recall the third and fourth movements and add labels ("Feet, stomach, feet, stomach, feet, stomach, feet, stomach"). Have children recall the first and second movements and then the third and fourth ones. Add all four movements with their labels to create a sequence ("Head, chin, feet, stomach").

Step 5

With the four volunteers facing the children, have the class "read" the children's movements and labels from left to right (head, chin, feet, stomach) and repeat the sequence as they SAY & DO. To simplify, have each volunteer only show his or her placement of hands, (e.g., the first child will leave his or her hands on his or her head).

K-Grade 2

Step 6

Start the steady beat; have the class repeat the four movements in steady beat; and then join in and SAY & DO the pattern, coming back to the beginning after they finish the last movement. Ask other children to volunteer and repeat the steps.

FACILITATION AND REFLECTION

★ How did you remember the sequence of movements?

★ Which sequence did you enjoy the most? Why?

★ Where else do you "read" from left to right?

EXTENSIONS

Preschool-Grade 2

★ Have the children represent the sequence with attribute blocks, and repeat the sequence several times. They can also string the sequence with wooden beads.

K-Grade 2

★ Make a class book of the sequences the children have made using digital photos.

★ Ask the children to find sequences in familiar stories or to tell the sequence of a familiar movie.

Grades 1-2

★ Encourage the children to perform their sequences of four places with music, using "Sauerländer Quadrille."

★ Have the children create a sequence that uses opposites such as "up, down," "in, out," or "push, pull," following the process in Step 4. Have the children find a partner, teach each other their sequence and the labels, and practice the first sequence and labels and then the second sequence and labels. Have the children SAY & DO the two sequences at least four times before adding "Sauerländer Quadrille." Combine the two sequences into a sequence of four movements (e.g., "in, out, push, pull"). Children SAY & DO their sequences before adding a few repetitions of "Sauerländer Quadrille" so the children can perform their sequence twice. Add the music again, letting it play longer so the children have about four to eight repetitions of their sequence. Have half of the partners perform their sequences to the music while the other half of the pairs watch and then change roles.

51

USING MOVEMENT TO UNDERSTAND a WEATHER GRAPH

Children choose movements to represent different types of weather, read a weather graph, and then represent the data through movement.

Movement & Music Curriculum Concepts
- Describing movement
- Moving in nonloco-motor ways

Literacy Curriculum Concepts
- Describing objects, events, and relations
- Reading graphs
- Using quantitative language

MATERIALS

★ Daily graph of the weather (see the sample graph included with this activity)

STEPS TO SUCCESS

K–Grade 2

Step 1

Ask the children to explore movements they could use to represent different kinds of weather.

Step 2

Ask a child to share his or her movement plan to represent a particular kind of weather. For example, one child might choose to represent rain and his plan might be showing his fingers floating in a downward motion. Have the other children join in, copy the child's plan, and describe how their bodies are moving and how the movement could represent a specific kind of weather. Another child might choose to represent rain in a different way and shares tapping her fingertips quickly on the floor. Have the other children copy, describe, and now compare and contrast the different ways of showing rain.

Step 3

Ask for volunteers to share their movement plans for other kinds of weather, and encourage them to describe their movement plan and how it represents weather.

Step 4

Have the children look at the classroom graph that represents weather each day so far for this month. Ask a volunteer to read the column showing windy days (each day recorded as windy is a shaded box). Ask another volunteer to suggest a movement to represent windy days, such as swaying side to side. Then ask children to plan their movement to represent the bar for windy weather on the graph. In this example, the movement planned to represent windy weather (swaying side to side) is done once for each day recorded as windy. In the sample graph, there are four boxes, so the children would repeat the movement four times.

Step 5

Have the children choose other movements to represent the other types of weather on the graph. The children should then look at the graph and repeat the chosen movement for the number of boxes on the bar for that particular weather. Ask the children questions such as "According to this weather graph, which kind of weather have we had the most of? The least of?" Have children compare the quantities on the graph using words such as *more, less, fewer,* and *the same*.

November Weather Graph

	sunny							
	cloudy							
	rainy							
	foggy							
	snowy							
	windy							

FaciLiTaTioN aND RefLecTioN

★ What is your favorite kind of weather? Why?

★ How did using movement help you to understand the information on the graph?

★ What did you notice when the quantities were more? Less? The same?

★ What other quantitative words could be used?

ExTeNSioNS

K-Grade 2

★ Graph and represent through movement the following: longer and shorter hours of daylight, sunrise/sunset, lunch count, attendance, growth, books read (comparing fiction and nonfiction), and so forth.

★ See Activity 18, related to duration.

Using Punctuation: Exclamation Points*

Children keep steady beat to and recite phrases about the exclamation point and its application by using movement to represent that exclamations end with exclamation points.

Movement & Music Curriculum Concepts
- Describing movement
- Feeling and expressing steady beat
- Moving in locomotor ways

Literacy Curriculum Concepts
- Editing
- Expressive reading
- Expressive speech
- Using punctuation

Materials

★ Chart paper or whiteboard

★ Markers or dry-erase markers

Steps to Success

K–Grade 2

Step 1

Write the exclamations from Step 2 on chart paper or the whiteboard. (You can also use exclamations that the children generated at another time.)

Step 2

Ask the children to look at the following exclamations (or exclamations that they have expressed at another time):

> This is fantastic!
> Look out below!
> That crocodile has huge teeth!

Read the exclamations together, and ask the children to look at them and tell a partner what they notice.

Teacher's Tip

Supporting the children in Step 5 means that you, as the teacher, model the problem solving and decision making that goes into knowing what punctuation could be used. Say, out loud, the examples in Step 2 using different intonations, and ask questions to help the children determine correct punctuation and their choice of movement.

---

*This activity is most appropriate for kindergartners when they are in the second half of the school year.

Step 3

Ask the children to march to a steady beat while you recite the following chant, joining in when they feel comfortable (note that the marching beat, which is the regular walking beat, is underlined):

Excla<u>ma</u>tion <u>points</u> <u>mean</u> you're <u>real</u>ly ex<u>ci</u>ted! _____ _____

March around the room (or in place) repeating this punctuation chant until most of the children are joining in. Lead a discussion with the class about what the punctuation chant means. Ask volunteers to show where it applies to the exclamations in Step 2.

Step 4

Ask the children to plan a way to represent an exclamation point at the end of an exclamation and describe their movement plan. For example, children might jump, spin 360 degrees, and yell "Woo!"

Step 5

Support the children as they reread an exclamation from Step 2 jumping, spinning, and yelling "Woo!" (or another movement chosen in Step 4) to represent the exclamation point. Then, as a class, march and repeat the punctuation chant.

Step 6

Write the following exclamation (or another child-generated exclamation) on chart paper or the whiteboard:

My kite is flying really high

Have the children read and respond with what needs to be fixed with this exclamation, and ask a volunteer to fix it on the chart paper or whiteboard.

Step 7

Ask the children to march and repeat the punctuation chant. Then help them read the exclamation from Step 6, adding the jump with a spin and "Woo!" (or another movement) to represent the exclamation point.

Step 8

Repeat Steps 6–7 with different exclamations so the children have many opportunities to recognize exclamations and to add the proper punctuation.

Facilitation and Reflection

★ How can you tell if you should use an exclamation point at the end of a sentence?

★ What does your voice do when you get to an exclamation point?

★ How can exclamation points help you with your reading and writing?

Extensions

K-Grade 2

★ Post the punctuation chant with the children's examples in a prominent place in your classroom.

★ Keep a list of child-generated exclamations for rereading and later use.

USING PUNCTUATION: PERIODS*

Children keep steady beat to and recite phrases about the period and its application by using movement to represent that sentences end with periods.

MATERIALS

★ Chart paper or whiteboard
★ Markers or dry-erase markers

STEPS TO SUCCESS

K–Grade 2

Step 1
Write the sentences from Step 2 on chart paper or the whiteboard. (You can also use sentences that the children generated at another time.)

Step 2
Ask the children to look at the following sentences (or sentences that they have generated at another time):

> Armani brought three packets of seeds.
> We can see small sprouts pushing through the dirt.
> These baby plants will need water everyday.

Read the sentences together, and ask the children to look at them and tell a partner what they notice.

---

*This activity is most appropriate for kindergartners when they are in the second half of the school year.

Step 3

Ask the children to march to a steady beat while you recite the following chant, joining in when they feel comfortable (note that the marching beat, which is the regular walking beat, is underlined):

Every sentence needs to end with a period. _____ _____

March around the room (or in place) repeating this punctuation chant until most of the children are joining in. Lead a discussion with the class about what the punctuation chant means. Ask volunteers to show where it applies to the sentences in Step 2.

Step 4

Ask the children to plan a way to represent the period at the end of any sentence and describe their movement plan. For example, children might stomp one foot loudly.

Step 5

Support the children as they reread a sentence from Step 2 stomping loudly with one foot (or another movement chosen in Step 4) to represent the period at the end of the sentence. Then, as a class, march and repeat the punctuation chant.

Step 6

Write the following sentence (or another child-generated sentence) on chart paper or the whiteboard:

Our plants will need sunlight, air, water, and food to grow strong

Have the children read and respond with what needs to be fixed with this sentence, and ask a volunteer to fix it on the chart paper or whiteboard.

Step 7

Ask the children to march and repeat the punctuation chant. Then help them read the sentence from Step 6 adding a loud stomp at the end of the sentence (or another movement) to represent the period.

Step 8

Repeat Steps 6–7 with different sentences so the children have many opportunities to recognize sentences and to add the proper punctuation.

Facilitation and Reflection

★ What happens at the end of a sentence?

★ How do you find the end of a sentence?

★ What does your voice do when you come to a period?

★ How do periods help you with your reading and writing?

Extensions

K-Grade 2

★ Post the punctuation chant and the children's examples in a prominent place in your classroom.

★ Keep a list of child-generated sentences for rereading and later use.

USING PUNCTUATION: QUESTION MARKS*

Children keep steady beat to and recite phrases about the question mark and its application by using movement to represent that questions end with question marks.

MATERIALS

★ Chart paper or whiteboard
★ Markers or dry-erase markers

STEPS TO SUCCESS

K–Grade 2

Step 1
Write the questions from Step 2 on chart paper or the whiteboard. (You can also use questions that the children generated at another time.) *Note:* The children will need to already understand that a question would require a response from someone.

Step 2
Ask the children to look at the following questions (or questions that they have generated at another time):

Can you recite your address?
When is it time for lunch?
What is your favorite color?

Read the questions together, and ask the children to look at them and tell a partner what they notice.

---

*This activity is most appropriate for kindergartners when they are in the second half of the school year.

Step 3

Ask the children to march to a steady beat while you recite the following chant, joining in when they feel comfortable (note that the marching beat, which is the regular walking beat, is underlined):

Every <u>question</u> <u>needs</u> to <u>end</u> <u>with</u> a <u>question</u> mark._____

March around the room (or in place) repeating this punctuation chant until most of the children are joining in. Lead a discussion with the class about what the punctuation chant means. Ask volunteers to show where it applies to the questions in Step 2.

Step 4

Ask the children to plan a way to represent the question mark at the end of any question and describe their movement plan. For example, children might lift both arms up as if to indicate "Huh?"

Step 5

Support the children as they reread a question from Step 2 lifting their arms up as if to indicate "Huh?" (or another movement chosen in Step 4). Then, as a class, march and repeat the punctuation chant.

Step 6

Write the following question (or another child-generated question) on chart paper or the whiteboard:

When will the tomatoes be ripe enough to eat

Help the children read and respond with what needs to be fixed with this question, and ask a volunteer to fix the question on the chart paper or whiteboard.

Step 7

Ask the children to march and repeat the punctuation chant. Then help them read the question from Step 6, adding the movement of lifting both arms up to indicate "Huh?" (or another movement) to represent the question mark.

Step 8

Repeat Steps 6–7 with different questions so the children have many opportunities to recognize questions and to add the proper punctuation.

Facilitation and Reflection

★ How can you tell if you need a question mark at the end of the sentence?

★ What does your voice do as you ask a question?

★ How do question marks help you with your reading and writing?

Extensions

K-Grade 2

★ Post the punctuation chant with the children's examples in a prominent place in your classroom.

★ Keep a list of child-generated questions for rereading and later use.

USING UPPERCASE LETTERS TO BEGIN SENTENCES*

Children keep steady beat to and recite phrases about punctuation and its application by using movement to represent that sentences begin with uppercase letters.

MATERIALS

★ Chart paper or whiteboard

★ Markers or dry-erase markers

STEPS TO SUCCESS

K–Grade 2

Step 1
Write the sentences from Step 2 on chart paper or the whiteboard. (You can also use sentences that the children generated at another time.)

Step 2
Ask the children to look at the following sentences (or sentences that they have generated at another time):

> The snails were sliding slowly.
> Our mealworms are now pupas.
> We found a grasshopper outside on the wall.

Read the sentences together, and ask the children to look at them and tell a partner what they notice.

---

*This activity is most appropriate for kindergartners when they are in the second half of the school year.

Step 3

Ask the children to march to a steady beat while you recite the following chant, joining in when they feel comfortable (note that the marching beat, which is the regular walking beat, is underlined):

You <u>al</u>ways <u>start</u> a <u>sen</u>tence <u>with</u> an <u>up</u>per<u>case</u> <u>let</u>ter. _____

March around the room (or in place) repeating this punctuation chant until most of the children have joined in. Lead a discussion with the class about what the punctuation chant means. Ask volunteers to show where it applies to the sentences in Step 2.

Step 4

Ask the children to plan a way to represent the first letter of any sentence and describe their movement plan. For example, children might stand up and stretch very tall.

Step 5

Support the children as they reread a sentence from Step 2 standing up and stretching tall to represent the uppercase letter at the beginning of each sentence (or another movement chosen in Step 4). Then, as a class, march and repeat the punctuation chant.

Step 6

Write the following sentence (or another child-generated sentence) on chart paper or the whiteboard:

it is a beautiful day.

Have the children read and respond with what needs to be fixed with this sentence, and ask a volunteer to fix it on the chart paper or whiteboard.

Step 7

Ask the children to march and repeat the punctuation chant. Then help them read the sentence from Step 6 by stretching up tall (or another movement) and reading "It is a beautiful day" to represent the change of the *i* to *I*.

Step 8

Repeat Steps 6–7 with different sentences so the children have many opportunities to recognize that sentences need to start with an uppercase letter.

FACILITATION AND REFLECTION

★ What happens at the beginning of a sentence?

★ How does that help you with your reading and writing?

EXTENSIONS

K–Grade 2

★ Post the punctuation chant with the children's examples in a prominent place in your classroom. Refer to it often.

VERBS SHOW ACTION*

Children explore different ways to move (actions) and then sing songs about their actions.

Movement & Music Curriculum Concepts
- Moving in locomotor ways
- Moving in nonlocomotor ways
- Singing songs

Literacy Curriculum Concepts
- Using verbs

MATERIALS

★ "Verbs Show Action" on the enclosed CD

★ CD player

★ A book that uses lots of action verbs. Some good examples include *Dragon Dancing* by Carole Schaefer, *Muncha! Muncha! Muncha!* by Candace Fleming, *Move!* by Robin Page and Steve Jenkins, and *Slide and Slurp, Scratch and Burp* by Brian Cleary (Extensions)

★ CD player

★ Chart paper or whiteboard (Extensions)

★ Markers or dry-erase markers (Extensions)

STEPS TO SUCCESS

K-Grade 2

Step 1
Ask the children to make a plan on a way to move. Have them carry out the movement plan and then share, describe, and label their actions with a partner.

---

*This activity is most appropriate for kindergartners when they are in the second half of the school year.

Step 2

Explore with the children the concept of verbs and how verbs show action. Ask the children to explore with a partner how many different kinds of activities they can do. Ask volunteers to share their movements while the rest of the class copies the movement and adds a label using SAY & DO (children *say* the words that define their actions [SAY] and they *match the movements to the words* [DO]). Comment on the movements as the children share them. Say, for example, "Yes, we are shaking our arms" or "Twist is an action. Another word for action is verb."

Step 3

Introduce "Verbs Show Action" (on the next page) to the tune of "Hot Cross Buns." (You can learn the song from the enclosed recording). See the sidebar on Learning New Songs for tips on how to start the children together.

Step 4

Ask for a volunteer to share his or her action while the rest of the group copies. Then add the song. For example, a volunteer might share pounding his or her hands. Have the class pound their hands, label the movement, and then sing (see verse 2 in "Verbs Show Action"). Continue the process with movement first, and then add the song.

Learning New Songs

Have the children start a movement in steady beat. Synchronize the movement by using an anchor word for each beat (e.g., "Beat, beat, beat, beat"). While keeping steady beat, say "Beat, beat, beat, listen," and sing the melody on a neutral syllable such as "bahm." Sing the melody several times on a neutral syllable, encouraging children to join in singing on a neutral syllable. Sing "Beat, beat, ready to sing" using the beginning pitch of the song (as demonstrated on the enclosed CD) and sing the song with the lyrics. As you repeat the song, ask the children to join in, singing the first verse of the song at least four times.

FACILITATION AND REFLECTION

★ What do you now know about verbs?

★ Why are they important in sentences or stories?

EXTENSIONS

K-Grade 2

★ Write down the verbs that the children suggest on chart paper or the whiteboard.

★ Write sentences or stories using the verbs on the chart paper or whiteboard.

★ Read a book to the children that uses a lot of action verbs (see the suggestions in the Materials section or the list of movement books at the end of the book for additional ideas). Have the children act out the action word (verb) from each page in the book. Ask volunteers to act out their favorite action word and then have the other children join in and identify the action word. Write down their favorite action words from the story, and have children use these words to create their own story.

Children explore different ways to move.

These children are sharing their movements with each other.

Verbs Show Action

(Hot Crossed Buns)

Verbs   show   ac - tion_____   Verbs   show   ac - tion_____

Verbs   show   ac - tions   That   we   can   all   do.

Verse 2

Pound our legs
Pound our legs
Pound is an action
That we can all do.

Verse 3

Twist our torso
Twist our torso
Twist is an action
That we can all do.

Verse 4

Jump in place
Jump in place
Jump is an action
That we can all do.

Verse 5

March in place
March in place
March is an action
That we can all do.

WATER CYCLE*

Children listen to the story of the water cycle and represent it through movement.

MATERIALS

★ Books about the water cycle, such as *The Drop Goes Plop* (by Sam Goodwin), *The Snow Flake: A Water Cycle Story* (by Neil Waldman), *Water Dance* (by Thomas Locker), and *Down Comes the Rain* by Franklyn M. Branley

★ Chart paper or whiteboard (dry-erase makers if using whiteboard)

★ Paper for children to write on

★ Writing instruments (pencils, markers, crayons, chalk, etc.)

STEPS TO SUCCESS

K–Grade 2

Step 1
Ask the children to brainstorm daily routine activities that they have to repeat again and again (e.g., put toothpaste on the brush, brush teeth, put toothbrush away, eat, put toothpaste on the brush, brush teeth, put toothbrush away, eat). Write down these ideas on chart paper or the whiteboard.

*This activity is most appropriate for kindergartners when they are in the second half of the school year.

Step 2

Have the children work with a partner, choose an activity from the chart paper or whiteboard, and then represent the activity in a circular drawing.

Step 3

Read a book to the class that describes the water cycle (see the suggestions in the Materials section).

Step 4

Begin narrating the story of the water cycle, stopping after describing each part of the cycle and encouraging the children to explore movements that represent the different parts of the water cycle. The following summary of the water cycle provides you with a framework of how to integrate movement as you narrate the story:

Evaporation: Evaporation begins with water molecules. Have the children make themselves very small and close together to represent water molecules in the ocean.

As the sun shines and heats up the water, the molecules begin to move more quickly. As they bounce and bump each other very gently, some get loose and separate from the others. These molecules are very light and begin to float into the air as a gas *(evaporation)*. Have the children represent floating into the air by vocalizing "Evaporation" with their singing voice rising as their body does.

Accumulation: After the water molecules rise, they begin to bump into other water molecules in gas or vapor form and begin to cling to each other and make clumps of gas that form a cloud. As the children represent the water vapor clinging and clumping through movement, have them use their singing voice to sing using random pitch and repeat "Accumulation, we're making a cloud" each time they attach to another child (another molecule).

Condensation: Because the atmosphere is thinner up high and does not hold heat as well as it does low at ground level, the clumps of gas continue to cool and cling. This changes the water vapor or gas back to the liquid state of water in the clouds. As the clouds get heavier and heavier, water droplets begin to make the cloud heavy *(condensation)*. Children can act out getting heavier as they clump together and use random pitch singing to sing about how the vapor is changing back to water by cooling off and condensing as it rises and clumps with other water vapor molecules.

Precipitation (rain, snow, or hail): As the clouds become heavier as they accumulate more water vapor, the water vapor begins to change to liquid and the water droplets begin to fall *(precipitation)*. Have children represent falling rain through movement, and sing their favorite song about rain.

(Please turn the page.)

Step 5

Choose songs about rain to share with the class, such as "Rain, Rain, Go Away," "It's Raining, It's Pouring," "Singing in the Rain," "I Love to Walk in the Rain," "Raindrops Keep Falling on My Head," "It Ain't Gonna Rain No More," or other songs that you and the children know.

Step 6

Have the children work together to record the water cycle on paper, with drawings, showing the water cycle labeled.

Step 7

Have the children create a four-movement sequence to represent the water cycle. Help them say the scientific name of each part of the water cycle as they do their movement sequence.

> **Singing Familiar Songs Together**
>
> Have children start a movement in steady beat. Synchronize the movement by using an anchor word for each beat (e.g., "Beat, beat, beat, beat"). Prepare the children to join in the song together by using the beginning pitch of the song to sing "Beat, beat, beat, sing" or "One, two, sing with me" and begin the song.

FACILITATION AND REFLECTION

★ How does this sequence show a cyclic event?

★ What are other examples of cyclic events (e.g., seasons, tides, phases of the moon, daily routines, life cycles, and so forth)?

★ What literature have you read that describes cyclic events? (Examples include *The Very Hungry Caterpillar* by Eric Carle and *Cloudy With a Chance of Meatballs* by Judi Barrett and Ron Barrett.)

EXTENSIONS

K-Grade 2

★ Help the children write and illustrate cyclic stories in the style of *If You Give a Mouse a Cookie* by Laura Joffe Numeroff.

★ Support the children as they write about and illustrate cyclic events that are nonfiction (e.g., seasons; tides; phases of the moon; daily routines; life cycle of insects, birds, or mammals; life cycle of plants).

★ Find poems about the rain and recite poetry with the class.

Once children have had the opportunity to explore a new topic through movement, they have experiences to draw on when putting pencil (or marker) to paper.

58

What Is It? Describing an Object's Attributes

Children choose an object in the classroom and describe its attributes through language and movement.

Movement & Music Curriculum Concepts
- Exploring vocal sounds
- Expressing creativity in movement
- Feeling and expressing steady beat
- Moving in locomotor ways

Literacy Curriculum Concepts
- Describing attributes
- Using descriptive language

Materials

★ Ordinary classroom objects
★ Paper bag for each child
★ Chart paper or whiteboard
★ Markers or dry-erase markers

Steps to Success

Preschool–Grade 2

Step 1
Without the children seeing, put a familiar classroom object in a paper bag and describe attributes of the object to the class.

Step 2
Support the children as they list on the chart paper or whiteboard (with words, icons, or both) attributes of the object, and reread the attributes as another is added. For example, you might say, "Let's see what we know so far. We know that the object is round like a sphere or a ball, it has a lot of blue on it, and it has lots of words on it." (In this example, the teacher has a miniature globe in the bag.)

Step 3
Show the object, and encourage the children to describe what they know about the object using complete sentences. At this point everyone will be speaking at the same time.

Step 4
Ask the children to plan a way to move their body and use a vocal sound to represent the object that has been described. For example, a child may spin in place and make vocal sounds that sound like the wind to represent the miniature globe and to show that the earth is spinning.

Step 5
Give each child a paper bag and the task of finding one object from the room to put in the bag.

Step 6
Ask the children to bring their bag with them to a meeting place and then ask a volunteer to share the attributes of the object (but not the name of the object). Ask the children to explore and make a plan on how to represent the object through movement and sound. Repeat with other volunteers as time allows.

K-Grade 2

Step 7
Ask the children to choose a partner. Have partners describe their object to each other and make a plan of how to represent each object through movement and sound. Ask the children to do their movement and sounds for each of their objects.

Step 8
Repeat Steps 6–7 so that the children have many opportunities to describe the object in their bag and to create plans to represent the object through movement and sound.

Facilitation and Reflection

★ What kinds of words did you use to describe your object?

★ How did you move?

★ What sounds did you make to represent your object?

> **TEACHER'S TIP**
>
> The objective is not for children to guess the object but to practice talking about the object. Teacher facilitation could be interjected to suggest other attributes, such as what the object is used for; where you would normally find it; how it moves; the sounds it makes; and its shape, color, size, texture, and material.

What's the Weather?

Children use movement to represent different kinds of weather, share and describe these movements with each other, and then create new lyrics to a familiar tune about the weather.

Materials

★ "What's the Weather?" on the enclosed CD

★ CD player

★ Index cards (Extensions)

★ Writing instruments (pencils, markers, crayons, etc.) (Extensions)

Steps to Success

K–Grade 2

Step 1
Sing the first two lines of "What's the Weather" to the tune of "London Bridge," replacing Tuesday with the correct day.

Step 2
Ask the children to explore ways to represent different kinds of weather through movement.

SAY & DO means that children *say* the words that define their actions (SAY) and they *match the movement to the words* (DO).

Step 3
Ask a volunteer to share his or her movement plan (e.g., one child waves both arms slowly from one side to the other to represent wind). Have the children copy the movement and describe it. Ask the volunteer to give it a label (e.g., windy). As a class SAY & DO the movement with the label of "Whoosh, whoosh, whoosh, whoosh."

Step 4

Have the children start a movement in steady beat and synchronize the movement by using an anchor word for each beat (e.g., "Beat, beat, beat, beat"). While keeping steady beat, say "Beat, beat, beat, and listen," and sing "What's the Weather" on a neutral syllable such as "bahm," encouraging the children to join in. Sing "Beat, beat, ready now to sing" using the beginning pitch of the song, and ask the children to join in as you sing the song several times.

Step 5

Ask the children to check outside to see if it is windy and, as a class, sing the answer to the question in the song.

Step 6

Have the children choose different kinds of weather to represent and sing about, repeating Steps 3–5.

FACILITATION AND REFLECTION

★ How did you decide which kinds of weather to represent?

★ How did you decide the movement you would use to represent that weather?

★ How did you come to a plan for each movement?

★ What are some things you would notice if the weather was windy? Snowy? Rainy?

EXTENSIONS

K-Grade 2

Have the children make a movement sequence to represent the weather for the day. For example, if the children said that it is cold, windy, and rainy, they would write those terms on three index cards and plan three movements to represent the day's weather. Have them rearrange the sequence and plan and do their own movement sequence, repeating their sequence many times. Ask for volunteers to perform for each other.

What's the Weather?
(London Bridge)

Verse 2

It is windy out today,
Out today, out today,

It is windy out today,
On this Tuesday.

WHEN TWO VOWELS GO WALKING*

Children explore vowel combinations and use movement to represent the rhyme: "When two vowels go walking, the first one does the talking and says its name."

MATERIALS

★ Large cards with one vowel printed on each

★ "Soldier's Joy" on the enclosed CD

★ CD player

★ Chart paper or whiteboard

★ Markers or dry-erase markers

STEPS TO SUCCESS

K–Grade 2

Step 1
Have the children work with a partner to explore various ways to move together sychronizing their movement and timing.

Step 2
Play "Soldier's Joy." Ask the partners to move together to the steady beat of "Soldier's Joy" for one repetition of the melody.

---

*This activity is most appropriate for kindergartners when they are in the second half of the school year.

Step 3

Ask the partners to plan a way to move together so that they are both moving forward with one in front and the other following but connected to the partner in front. The partner who is in front sets the timing of their movement.

Step 4

Using the movement in Step 3, have the partners travel with "Soldier's Joy" for a repetition of the melody. Then have them switch roles so that the other one is in front.

Step 5

Ask the partners to switch roles again, but this time, ask the child in front to say his or her name with each step. The partner following is silent but matches the movement of the person in front. Then have the partners switch roles.

Step 6

Ask a child to volunteer to be your partner, and you and your partner each hold a vowel card. Traveling forward and connected (that is, holding hands), say the name of the vowel on the card out loud that you are holding, saying the vowel name with each step. Your partner behind matches the movement but remains silent. For example, if you are in front and holding a vowel card that has an *e* on it and the partner is holding a vowel card with an *a* on it, you would start moving forward and then say, "E, e, e, e," repeating one letter for each step taken. Your partner is silent but matches your movements.

Making Connections

The two vowels (and children) are working together by moving together. The first one is saying its name, just like in the rhyme (note that the marching beat is underlined):

> "When <u>two</u> <u>vo</u>wels go <u>wal</u>king, _____
> the <u>first</u> one <u>does</u> the <u>tal</u>king _____
> and <u>says</u> <u>its</u> <u>name</u> _____."

The sound of the letter being spoken by the first child as they work together (or move together) is a concrete representation of an abstract concept.

Step 7

Trade roles with your partner. This time, as in the example, the *a* is in front and the *e* is behind. The child with the *a* will say *a* with each step, and you, holding the *e,* are silent but match the movement of the first child.

Step 8

Ask all the children to pick a vowel card and a partner and complete Steps 6–7. Then ask them to choose new partners (but keep the same cards) and repeat Steps 6–7 so that the children are exploring strategies to pronounce words with vowel combinations.

Step 9

With the class, brainstorm and write down words on chart paper or the whiteboard that have two vowels "walking" together (e.g., *Jean, brain, read, toe, clue*).

Step 10

Act out each set of two vowels from the words, adding the rhyme "When <u>two</u> <u>vo</u>wels go <u>walk</u>ing, ___ the <u>first</u> one <u>does</u> the <u>talk</u>ing ___ and <u>says</u> <u>its</u> <u>name</u>" to help the children remember this commonly known rule. For example, each child has a partner to work with and each child decides which vowel of the combination he or she would take as his or her role. Taking the name *Jean* off of the chart, partners walk together with the whole group in synchronization, reciting, "When two vowels go walking, the first one does the talking and says its name." Then, add the *ea* combination so that following the rule would be spoken as "ē, ē, ē, ē, ē, ē, ē," repeat-

ing one letter for each step. The first person says *e* while the partner taking the role of the *a* is matching the movement but is silent. Go back to *Jean,* and say *Jean* on each march eight times: "Jean, Jean, Jean, Jean, Jean, Jean, Jean, Jean."

Step 11
Repeat Step 10 with other words from the chart or whiteboard in Step 9.

Step 12
Search environmental print, storybooks, and science books to find words with two vowels together and to see which words follow this. Use these words to work through Step 10.

FaciLitation and Reflection

★ How can this strategy help you when you come to a word that you don't know that has two vowels next to each other?

Extensions

K-Grade 2

★ Create a word bank of words that have two vowels "walking" together. List them by vowel combination (*ai* words together, *ea* words together, *oe* words together, etc.).

MOVEMENT BOOKS

We have used these books in our classrooms; however, this list is in no way complete, as we add to it on a regular basis as we discover other books that lend themselves to the representation of text through movement.

Giles Andreae	*Giraffes Can't Dance*
Kathi Appelt	*Incredible Me!*
Molly Bang	*When Sophie Gets Angry*
Mikhail Baryshnikov	*Because*
Sandra Boynton	*Barnyard Dance*
Megan Bryant	*Just Like Daddy*
	Just Like Mommy
Caralyn Buehner	*Snowmen at Night*
Ann Burg	*Autumn Walk*
Lorinda Bryan Cauley	*Clap Your Hands*
Eric Carle	*From Head to Toe*
	Slowly, Slowly, Said the Sloth
	The Very Busy Spider
Lauren Child	*Charlie & Lola's Opposites*
Vicki Churchill & Charles Fuge	*Sometimes I Like to Curl Up in a Ball*
Emma Chichester Clark	*Follow the Leader!*
Brian Cleary	*Slide and Slurp, Scratch and Burp*
Jamie Lee Curtis	*Today I Feel Silly and Other Moods*
	That Make My Day
Olivier Dunrea	*Gossie*
Joe Ewers	*Clap Your Hands*
Candace Fleming	*Muncha! Muncha! Muncha!*
Denise Fleming	*In the Tall, Tall Grass*
Michael Grejniec	*What Do You Like?*
Bell Hooks	*Be Boy Buzz*
Rachel Isadora	*Max*
	On Your Toes: A Ballet ABC
Ezra Jack Keats	*Over in the Meadow*
	The Snowy Day
Patricia Lakin	*Snow Day!*
Spike Lee & Tonya Lewis Lee	*Please, Baby, Please*
Gina Lems-Tardif	*Pilgrim Children Had Many Chores*
Kevin Lewis	*Chugga-chugga Choo-choo*
Christine Kale MacLean	*Even Firefighters Hug Their Moms*
Bill Martin, Jr.	*Brown Bear, Brown Bear, What Do You See?*
Tony Mitton	*Down by the Cool of the Pool*
Jane O'Connor	*Ready, Set, Skip!*
Jan Ormerod	*If You're Happy and You Know It!*
Robin Page & Steve Jenkins	*Move!*
Raffi Songs to Read	*Shake My Sillies Out*
Phyllis Root	*One Duck Stuck*
Carole Lexa Schaefer	*Dragon Dancing*

Dr. Seuss	*My Many Colored Days*
Irene Smalls	*Jonathan and His Mommy*
Ellen Stoll Walsh	*Hop Jump*
Linda Williams	*The Little Old Lady Who Was Not Afraid of Anything*
Sue Williams	*I Went Walking*
Audrey Wood	*Quick as a Cricket*

Steady Beat Books

The following books can be read while the children rock or quietly pat to the steady beat. The text should be read using a natural flow of speech (not sing-song) and is layered on top of the steady beat. Be sure to stop and anchor the beat many times throughout the piece of literature, as demonstrated on the enclosed CD (listen to "The Gingerbread Man" and "The Old Lady Who Swallowed the Fly"). This gives the children another opportunity to match the steady beat with one-to-one correspondence and feel the beat and underlying pulse of the text.

Poetry Picks

Alan Katz	*I'm Still Here in the Bathtub*
Bruce Lansky	*A Bad Case of the Giggles*
	Kids Pick the Funniest Poems
	My Dog Ate My Homework
Judy Lalli	*I Like Being Me*
Mother Goose rhymes and poems	
Jack Prelutsky	*For Laughing Out Loud*
	The Frogs Wore Red Suspenders
	A Pizza the Size of the Sun
	Ride a Purple Pelican
	Scranimals
Shel Silverstein	*Falling Up*
	A Light in the Attic
	Where the Sidewalk Ends
Eloise Wilkins	*Poems to Read to the Very Young*

Steady Beat in Children's Picture Books

Kathi Appelt	*Bats Around the Clock*
Jim Aylesworth	*Old Black Fly*
Teresa Bateman	*April Foolishness*
Felicia Bond	*Tumble Bumble*
Tony Bradman	*Daddy's Lullaby*
Eve Bunting	*Sing a Song of Piglets*
Jamie Lee Curtis	*I'm Gonna Like Me*
Bruce Degen	*Jamberry*
Diane & Leo Dillon	*Rap a Tap Tap*
Kin Eagle	*It's Raining, It's Pouring*
	Rub a Dub Dub
	Humpty Dumpty
Ella Fitzgerald	*A-Tisket, A-Tasket*
Elaine Good	*Fall Is Here! I Love It!*
Woody Guthrie	*This Land Is Your Land*

Will Hillenbrand	*Down by the Station*
Judy Hindley	*Do Like a Duck Does!*
Mary Ann Hoberman	*Miss Mary Mack*
	The Lady With the Alligator Purse
Mary Howitt	*The Spider and the Fly*
Alison Jackson	*I Know an Old Lady Who Swallowed a Pie*
Robert Kalan	*Jump, Frog, Jump*
Buddy Kaye, Fred Wise, & Sidney Lippman	*A You're Adorable*
David Kirk	*Little Miss Spider*
	Little Miss Spider at Sunny Patch School
Edward Lear	*Hilary Knight's the Owl and the Pussy Cat*
Reeve Lindbergh	*My Hippie Grandmother*
Henry Wadsworth Longfellow	*Paul Revere's Ride*
Bill Martin, Jr., & John Archambault	*Chicka Chicka Boom Boom*
Dave McPhail	*Those Can-Do Pigs*
Shirley Neitzel	*The Dress I'll Wear to the Party*
W. Nikola-Lisa	*Shake dem Halloween Bones*
Tom Paxton	*Going to the Zoo*
Raffi Songs to Read	*Baby Beluga*
	Down by the Bay
	Five Little Ducks
	Spider on the Floor
Iza Trapani	*I'm a Little Teapot*
Rick Walton	*Bunnies on the Go*
George David Weiss & Bob Thiele	*What a Wonderful World*
Nancy Van Laan & George Booth	*Possum Come a-Knockin'*
Michael Wenberg	*Elizabeth's Song*
Linda Williams	*The Little Old Lady Who Was Not Afraid of Anything*
Natasha Wing	*The Night Before Kindergarten*

Vocal Exploration Books

These books encourage children to explore how they can approximate the sounds using their own voices.

Eric Carle	*The Very Quiet Cricket*
Betsy Franco	*Summer Beat*
Marla Frazee	*Roller Coaster*
Judy Hindley	*Does a Cow Say Boo?*
Pat Hutchins	*Good-Night, Owl!*
Charles Reasoner	*Who Drives This?*
Michael Rosen	*We're Going on a Bear Hunt*
Dr. Seuss	*Gerald McBoing Boing*
	Mr. Brown Can Moo! Can You?
Arnold Shapiro	*Mice Squeak, We Speak*

WORDLESS PICTURE BOOKS

You can use these books to encourage children to sing (using random pitch) to tell the story that they see in the illustrations. Children can also use their singing voice to retell any story by describing what is happening in the illustrations.

Alexandra Day	*Carl Goes to Day Care*
	Carl's Afternoon in the Park
	Carl's Birthday
	Carl's Christmas
	Good Dog, Carl
Paul Fleischman & Kevin Hawkes	*Sidewalk Circus*
Mercer Mayer	*A Boy, a Dog, and a Frog*
Peggy Rathmann	*Good Night, Gorilla*
Peter Sis	*Dinosaur!*
Nancy Tafuri	*Have You Seen My Duckling?*
David Wiesner	*Tuesday*

GLOSSARY

active learning approach An educational perspective in which the teacher both introduces ideas and recognizes opportunities to support and extend ideas initiated by the learners.

alliteration The repetition of the same sounds, especially at the beginning of words.

alternating movements Movement in which two corresponding body parts take turns. For example, the two feet take turns in walking.

anchor word (pitch) A single word spoken or sung by the leader four or eight times to bring the group to beat synchronization before saying a rhyme or singing a song. Singing this word on the beginning pitch of the song *(anchor pitch)* enables the group to begin with a common beat and pitch.

anchored movement Having some part of the body in fixed contact with the surface (floor or ground) while other body parts move.

antonyms Words that have opposite meanings (e.g., light and dark).

approximation The act or process of being nearly the same as.

asymmetrical movement Movement in which two corresponding or two different body parts move at the same time in different ways.

aural The modality in which a learner listens, processes, and responds to spoken or sung directions.

basic timing Ability to independently feel and maintain the underlying steady beat of a rhyme, song, or recorded/live musical selection with nonlocomotor and locomotor movement. This ability is the intended outcome of the key developmental indicator *feeling and expressing steady beat*.

beat (steady beat) The consistent, repetitive pulse that lies within every rhyme, song, or musical selection. The pulse has even durations and occurs at equal intervals.

beat competence Demonstrated proficiency expressing and maintaining microbeat and/or macrobeat with nonlocomotor or locomotor movement while moving, singing, or playing instruments.

beat coordination Ability to perform sequences of movement to one's own steady beat and with others. This ability is the intended objective of the key developmental indicator *moving in sequences to a common beat*.

body awareness Understanding how each body part can move and what movement relationships exist among body parts.

cinquain A five-line stanza that can be expressed in different patterns. The simplest pattern for cinquain poetry has one word for the first and fifth lines, two words for the second line, three words for the third line, and four words for the fourth line.

cognitive Having to do with the process of mental learning or understanding.

concept An abstract idea fundamental to a specific body of knowledge.

creative movement Taking a movement that is familiar and changing it in some way.

direction An extension of movement that refers to where movement is going (upward/downward, forward/backward, sideward, around, clockwise/counterclockwise).

dynamic movement Movement that continues without pausing until the designated stopping point.

even timing Repeated movement having equal time intervals between the movements.

exploration Providing opportunities for the learner to take time to work in his or her own space and timing with a new concept.

facilitate A component of the Teaching Model in which the teacher uses varied strategies involving action, thought, and language to engage learners and enable them to construct their own knowledge.

fine-motor movement Movements and coordinations of movements performed with small-muscle groups.

form The organization or structure of a musical selection. For example, a selection can be in AB form, in AABB form, and so on.

gallop An uneven locomotor movement in which one foot is the leader and the other foot comes up to meet it.

general space All the available space within some large perimeter, such as the walls of a room or the boundaries of a playing field or court — all the space that a person can reach using locomotor movement.

gross-motor movement Movement (locomotor or nonlocomotor) of large-muscle groups.

hands-on-guidance Interacting with the learner by using the tactile/kinesthetic mode.

hop A locomotor movement that transfers weight from one foot to the same foot.

homonym One of two or more words that share the same sound and often the same spelling but have different meanings.

intensity An extension of movement that concerns how much force is applied.

internal timing The ability to feel a sense of steady pulse.

jump A locomotor movement that transfers weight from one or two feet to two feet. The landing is on two feet.

key developmental indicators The building blocks of thinking and reasoning at each stage of a child's development.

kinesthetic Pertaining to the processing and awareness of body movements.

language awareness An understanding of the labels associated with parts and actions of the body.

layering The process of starting a movement and then adding a word, rhyme, song, or recording.

level An extension of movement that shows whether the movement is in a low, middle, or high plane.

locomotor movement Nonanchored movement with transfers of weight in personal or general space (running, jumping, hopping, skipping, marching, climbing).

macrobeat* The rocking or patting beat that organizes groups of two or three microbeats, the first beat of each group of two or three microbeats.

microbeat* The regular walking beat; each beat of a group of two or three beats.

midline Crossing the midline is the ability to move one hand, foot, or eye into the space of the other hand, foot, or eye (e.g., patting your left shoulder with your right hand, reading left to right, or crossing your ankles).

---

*For more information about **macrobeat** and **microbeat**, see E. Gordon, *Learning Sequences in Music* (Chicago: GIA Publishing, 2003).

nonanchored movement Movement performed while no part of the body is in fixed contact with the floor, as in weight transfers.

nonlocomotor movement Anchored movement performed in one's own space without complete transfers of weight (bending, twisting, rocking, swinging one's arms).

one side...other side Repeated movement of one arm, leg, or hand, without moving the opposite arm, leg, or hand. This is followed by doing the same repeated movements with the corresponding body part on the opposite side.

pathway An on-the-floor or in-the-air pattern (straight, curved, zigzag) that the body creates with locomotor or nonlocomotor movement.

personal space All the space that any part of the body can reach while the body is anchored (when performing nonlocomotor movement).

phrase A musical (or spoken) thought that is part of a melody. One often stops to take a breath at the end of a phrase.

purposeful movement Movement that requires conscious thought on the part of the mover. It is planned beforehand; it can be labeled, recalled, and discussed.

random pitch singing Singing without a specified melody. It is a precursor to singing real melodies. Random pitch singing provides vocal exploration with the freedom to change pitches at random (there is no right or wrong way).

representation Movement that reenacts familiar actions or happening or imitates various living things and creatures. It involves moving "like" or "as if."

rhythm The pattern created by the durations of note values, words, or syllables within and among the beats of a rhyme, song, or musical selection.

rock A nonlocomotor movement that maintains the body in anchored position but partially shifts weight side-to-side or front-to-back.

SAY & DO The process whereby a learner says a word and simultaneously performs a related movement, creating a cognitive-motor link.

separate Involves using only one mode of presentations — visual demonstration, spoken directions, or hands-on-guidance — when presenting information to learners. This is a component of the Teaching Model.

sequenced movement Two or more purposeful movements (such as bending and straightening the arms) joined together; once it is completed, the sequence can repeat itself.

shape The appearance of a movement — whether it looks symmetrical, narrow, wide, curved, and so on.

simplify A component of the Teaching Model in which the teacher begins with what is manageable for the learner. This may mean breaking a task into subtasks.

single movement One movement that is held or repeated (e.g., patting knees, stomping one foot, or stepping).

size An extension of movement that refers to whether it is large, medium, or small.

skip An uneven locomotor movement that is the combination of two different transfers of weight — gallop and hop. Skipping has uneven timing.

slide An uneven locomotor movement, which may be thought of as a sideward gallop.

space awareness Understanding the "where" and "how" of movement, the body's relationship to personal and general space.

static movement Movement that stops or pauses before a new movement is presented.

steady beat The consistent repetitive pulse that lies within every rhyme, song, or musical selection.

swing A nonlocomotor movement that involves either forward-and-backward or side-to-side movement.

symmetrical movement Two (both) sides of the body doing the same movement at the same time.

synchronization To cause sound effects or dialogue to coincide with an action at the same time.

synonym A word having a meaning similar to the meaning of another word.

Teaching Model A presentation method consisting of three components — **separate, simplify,** and **facilitate.** The Teaching Model is fundamental to the "Education Through Movement" program's **active learning approach.**

tempo The speed of the song, rhyme, or musical selection.

time awareness The ability to understand whether a movement is fast/slow, even/uneven, or so on. All movement has timing.

tracking The act of visually following a movement.

turn A nonlocomotor movement that involves taking the arm or leg all the way around in a 360-degree movement; a locomotor movement that changes the facing direction.

two sides Corresponding body parts moving at the same time.

uneven timing When there are varied intervals of time between movements.

SUBJECT INDEX

A
Accents, 40, 72

Alliteration, 30, 58

Attributes, 12, 116, 146

Aural discrimination, 28, 34, 56

B
Books, 14, 86, 96, 98, 110, 118, 142

  characters in, 14, 54

  class, 54, 84, 86, 88, 126

C
Charts, 70, 86, 120

Classification, 76, 94

Compare/contrast, 74, 98, 116, 128

Consonant

  blends, 58, 62

  sounds, 30, 58, 60

Creativity

  expressing, 14, 26, 44, 64, 74, 96

E
Editing, 130, 132, 134, 136

G
Graphs, 50, 128

I
Ideas

  expression of, 38, 46, 54, 94, 104

L
Language

  descriptive, 42, 64, 70, 74, 86, 110, 116, 146, 148

  foreign, 48

  quantitative, 128

Letters, 20, 24, 52, 58, 62, 66, 72, 82, 116, 150

  shapes of, 20

M
Movement

  describing, 38, 42, 46, 52, 60, 68, 74, 98, 124

  locomotor, 12, 14, 20, 26, 38, 46, 58, 68, 74, 76, 84, 120, 138

  nonlocomotor, 18, 34, 42, 44, 62, 68, 74, 120, 124, 138

N
Names, 30, 46, 72

O
Opposites, 78, 124, 126

P
Pathways, 20, 24, 52, 62, 82

Phonemic awareness, 28, 34, 40, 150

Poetry, 74, 84, 86, 118

Positional words, 18, 38, 46, 88

Predictions, 16

Punctuation, 26, 104, 106, 130, 132, 134, 136

R
Reading, 86, 96, 98, 126, 136, 150

  expressive, 130, 132, 134, 136

Representation, 42, 44, 58, 70, 86, 110, 128

Rhymes, 30, 100

S
Same/different, 30, 62, 76

Sentences, 26, 38, 54, 60, 64, 104, 132, 134, 136, 148

Sequencing, 22, 28, 44, 68, 76, 88, 96, 106, 126, 142, 148

Singing, 34, 46, 48, 78, 88, 100, 106, 110, 114, 138, 142, 148

  random pitch, 16, 96

Sounds, 28, 34, 40, 50, 58, 60, 62, 66, 70, 86

Speech

  articulation, 28, 50

  expressive, 130, 132, 134

Steady beat, 12, 30, 34, 40, 48, 72, 84, 110, 118, 120, 126, 130, 132, 134, 136, 142, 148, 150

Stories

  dictating, 28, 84

  making up, 94

  retelling, 14, 56, 96

  writing, 22

Syllables, 40, 72

Synonyms/antonyms, 78, 124

V
Verbs, 58, 138

Visual tracking, 92, 126

Vocabulary,

  building, 12, 48, 70, 114, 142

Vocal

  expression, 50, 70

  sounds, 14, 28, 34, 50, 56, 66, 70, 84

Vowels

  double, 150

  sounds of, 150

W
Writing, 18, 22, 24, 42, 44, 46, 52, 54, 62, 70, 74, 76, 78, 84, 86, 88, 94, 98, 100, 104, 110, 120, 124, 138, 142, 148, 150

MUSICAL SELECTIONS PROVIDED WITH THIS BOOK.

The following selections appear on the CD included with this book. Suggestions for appropriate activities are given for each selection.

SELECTIONS ON CD

1. *The Ants Go Marching*
2. *B A Bay*
3. *The Beanbag Song*
4. *Cherkessiya*
5. *Ending Punctuation*
6. *Fee Fi Fiddly I O*
7. *The Gingerbread Man*
8. *Hello Friends*
9. *Hole in the Wall*
10. *Joe Clark Mixer*
11. *Jungle Beat*
12. *The Old Lady Who Swallowed the Fly*
13. *One, Two, Three*
14. *Opposites to the Tune of Looby Lu*
15. *People in Our Town*
16. *Popcorn*
17. *Raking All the Leaves*
18. *Random Pitch Singing*
19. *Road to the Isles*
20. *The Sally Gardens*

21. *Sally Go Round the Sun*
22. *Sauerländer Quadrille*

23. *Seed to Plant*
24. *Soldier's Joy*

25. *Verbs Show Action*
26. *What's the Weather?*
27. *Willaby Wallaby Woo*
28. *Yankee Doodle*

SUGGESTED ACTIVITIES

41. Rhyming Words With "The Ants Go Marching"
10. Exploring Alliteration
36. Positional Words With Beanbag Sequences
46. Statue Clones; 48. Steady Beat Warm-Up Chart
43. Sing a Song About Punctuation
10. Exploring Alliteration
47. Steady Beat Stories
17. Hello in Many Languages
25. Making Moving to Music Meaningful
48. Steady Beat Warm-Up Chart
11. Exploring Mouth Sounds
47. Steady Beat Stories
4. Creating My Own Song
32. Opposites
34. People in Our Town
25. Making Moving to Music Meaningful
44. Singing About the Seasons
3. Conversations Sung on Random Pitches
44. Singing About the Seasons
1. Attributes of Shapes;
7. Drawing Pathways, Shapes, and Letters;
25. Making Moving to Music Meaningful;
49. Synonyms and Antonyms
16. Getting In, Out, and Around
1. Attributes of Shapes;
50. Tracking in Sequences
15. From Seed to Plant
1. Attributes of Shapes; 46. Statue Clones;
48. Steady Beat Warm-Up Chart;
60. When Two Vowels Go Walking
56. Verbs Show Action
59. What's the Weather?
10. Exploring Alliteration
48. Steady Beat Warm-Up Chart;
49. Synonyms and Antonyms

ABOUT THE AUTHORS

Lizabeth Haraksin-Probst has been an educator in the Southern California area since 1983, teaching early elementary students as well as adults. Her focus for the past 18 years has been studying with Phyllis Weikart and implementing concepts from "Education Through Movement: Building the Foundation" in her classroom routine. She also shares this information with adults in local school districts; through University of California, Riverside, Extension courses; and as a Field Consultant for the Movement and Music Department of the High/Scope Educational Research Foundation. In 1998, Liz was nominated for the prestigious Bravo Award, given by the Music Center of the Los Angeles County.

Janet Hutson-Brandhagen has been an educator for 40 years. She began her teaching career as an elementary school and music teacher in Torrence, California. She then taught music at the preschool, elementary, and middle school level in Bellevue, Washington, for 31 years and served as the music curriculum developer and trainer for 15 years in Bellevue elementary schools. Her work with Phyllis Weikart has been the most valuable to her development as an educator — using the movement-based active learning approach has given her the greatest success with her students. Janet is currently a Field Consultant for the Movement and Music Department of the High/Scope Educational Research Foundation. In addition to High/Scope training workshops, she also presents workshops at conventions for All-Northwest and the Washington Music Educators Association.

Phyllis S. Weikart is Senior Advisor of the Movement and Music Department of the High/Scope Educational Research Foundation. She conducts training workshops and conference sessions for music, physical education, and early childhood educators through-out the United States. She is the author of 13 books about movement, music, and dance at all levels and is the producer of eight videos and 15 CDs. Her wide-ranging experiences have led to the development of a teaching approach that ensures teachers' success with students of all ages.

Resources From High/Scope

Round the Circle: Key Experiences in Movement for Young Children, 2nd Ed.

Young children learn through play, and their play is full of movement experiences. *Round the Circle* has been completely revised to present the *High/Scope Education Through Movement: Building the Foundation* program for preschoolers developed by Phyllis S. Weikart. This second edition presents *eight key experiences in movement* that help adults *engage, enable,* and *extend* children's active movement explorations. In addition, Weikart's teaching model provides a strong framework for encouraging and supporting young children's learning. Readers will appreciate the numerous *suggested activities, concrete guidelines,* and *effective teaching strategies* that are peppered throughout the book. Use this well-illustrated and easy-to-understand book to make the most of children's movement adventures!

BK-M1020
P. S. Weikart. Soft cover, 176 pages. 1-57379-096-6

Movement in Steady Beat — Learning on the Move, Ages 3 to 7, 2nd Ed.

The activities in this book will keep young children moving to the beat — and loving it! Infant-toddler caregivers as well as preschool and early elementary teachers will welcome the learning experiences that develop children's basic timing, language, vocabulary, concentration, decision making, and leadership abilities. The attached CD contains rhymes and action song recordings for many of the book's activities.

BK-M1023
P. S. Weikart. Soft cover, 108 pages, includes music CD. 1-57379-130-X

Movement Plus Music: Activities for Children Ages 3 to 7, 3rd Ed.

This revised and expanded book of activities and accompanying CD will enable you to provide many opportunities for children to experience the fun and creativity of music. While enjoying these activities, children will develop key abilities that are foundations both for physical and academic learning: steady beat competence, physical coordination, concentration, and the ability to process information and act on it. Eight basic activities are presented, with many variations for each. The activities may be used at group times, at transition times, or in outdoor group activities.

BK-M1027
P. S. Weikart. Soft cover, 36 pages, illustrated, includes music CD. 1-57379-214-4

Movement Plus Rhymes, Songs, & Singing Games, 2nd Ed.

A revised collection of engaging movement activities for children. These activities supplement those described in *Round the Circle* and provide age-appropriate movement experiences. Use them during large-group time, small-group time, or transitions. Includes CD with colorful, appropriate music to accompany activities.

BK-M1025
P. S. Weikart. Soft cover, 100 pages, includes music CD. 1-57379-066-4

Order online: *www.highscope.org*

High/Scope Preschool Key Experiences Series: Movement and Music

This booklet and video program provides a roadmap of how movement and music abilities develop in young children and how adults can support this process. Included are eight movement key experiences and six music key experiences. Through these experiences children develop steady beat competence, physical coordination, concentration, and the ability to process information and act on it. This informative booklet and colorful video provide many examples of children engaging in fun-filled activities that promote their development in movement and music. Also covered are many strategies teachers can use to support learning in these areas during teacher-planned group times and transition times, as well as during children's spontaneous play both indoors and outside.

Book: BK-P1244, Video: BK-P1245, DVD: BK-P1304,
Book & Video Set: BK-P1246SET, Book & DVD Set: BK-P1314SET
Book, soft cover, photos, 36 pages, 1-57379-210-1. Video, color, 79 minutes, viewer guide included. 1-57379-211-X. DVD, 1-57379-277-2

85 Engaging Movement Activities — Learning on the Move, K–6

The activities in this book will keep your K–6 students jogging, hopping, swaying, rocking, marching, patting, making pathways, and moving in all kinds of ways as they learn. Classroom teachers, as well as specialty teachers in physical education, music, and recreation, will find this book to be a rich source of ideas for challenging and enjoyable movement experiences. The experiences are planned around key curriculum concepts in movement and music as well as in academic curriculum areas such as math and reading. And because these experiences develop students' basic timing, language abilities, vocabulary, concentration, planning skills, and capabilities for cooperative decision making and leadership, teachers will see learning effects that stretch across the curriculum. An easy-to-follow plan is given for each activity. The attached music CD contains recordings that may be used with many of the activities from this book.

BK-E3040
P. S. Weikart and E. B. Carlton. Soft cover, illustrated, 216 pages, includes music CD. 1-57379-125-3

75 Ensemble Warm-Ups: Activities for Bands, Choirs, and Orchestras — Learning on the Move, Grades 4–12

The newest addition to the Learning on the Move series, this book is a resource for conductors and directors of a variety of vocal and instrumental ensembles — from upper elementary choirs, Orff ensembles, and beginning bands to middle school and high school choirs, orchestras, and bands.

These active start-ups to ensemble rehearsals will result in more productive sessions as students explore, share, discuss, and discover the information necessary to be self-directed musicians. For grades 4–12. Free music CD included with book.

BK-M1024
P. S. Weikart, B. Boardman, & E. Bryant. Soft cover, 216 pages, CD included. 1-57379-144-X

Order online: *www.highscope.org*